Cicero: De Imperio

Bloomsbury Latin Texts

Other titles in the series:

Cicero: *In Catilinam I and II*, edited by J. L. Whiteley
9780862920142

Cicero: *Philippics I–II*, edited by J. D. Denniston
9780906515082

Cicero: *Pro Milone*, edited by F. H. Colson
9780906515501

Cicero: *Pro Roscio Amerino*, edited by E. H. Donkin
9780862921842

Cicero: De Imperio

An Extract: 27–45

Notes and vocabulary by
Katharine Radice
Introduction by Catherine Steel

Bloomsbury Academic
An Imprint of Bloomsbury Publishing Plc

B L O O M S B U R Y
LONDON • NEW DELHI • NEW YORK • SYDNEY

Bloomsbury Academic

An imprint of Bloomsbury Publishing Plc

50 Bedford Square	1385 Broadway
London	New York
WC1B 3DP	NY 10018
UK	USA

www.bloomsbury.com

**BLOOMSBURY and the Diana logo are trademarks of
Bloomsbury Publishing Plc**

First published 2014
Reprinted by Bloomsbury Academic 2014

British Library Cataloguing-in-Publication Data
A catalogue record for this book is available from the British Library.

ISBN: PB: 978-1-4725-1117-1
ePDF: 978-1-4725-1376-2
ePub: 978-1-4725-1121-8

Library of Congress Cataloging-in-Publication Data
Cicero, Marcus Tullius, author.
[Pro lege Manilia]
De imperio : a selection: 27-45 / Cicero ; introduction by Catherine Steel ;
commentary, notes and vocabulary by Katharine Radice.
pages cm
Includes bibliographical references and index.
ISBN 978-1-4725-1117-1 (pbk.) – ISBN 978-1-4725-1121-8 (epub) –
ISBN 978-1-4725-1376-2 (epdf) 1. Cicero, Marcus Tullius. Pro lege Manilia.
I. Radice, Katharine. II. Title.
PA6279.I6 2014
875'.01–dc23
2013036179

Series: Latin Texts

Typeset by Fakenham Prepress Solutions, Fakenham, Norfolk NR21 8NN
Printed and bound in Great Britain

Contents

Maps

THE EASTERN
MEDITERRANEAN

THE ROMAN WORLD

A N I A

S A R M A T I A

Cimmerian Bosporus

B L A C K   S E A

COLCHIS

YRICUM

Sea

THRACE

Bosporus

PONTUS

Trapezus

MACEDONIA
Brundisium

BITHYNIA

ARMENIA

Pharsalus

Pergamum
A S I A
C. Corycus

CAPPADOCIA

Chaeronea
Corinth
Athens
Delos

ACHAIA

Aegean Sea

Isauria
PAMPHYLIA *CILICIA*

Tigranocerta •

A N E A N   S E A

CRETE

CYPRUS

SYRIA

CYRENAICA

EGYPT

Preface

This edition is designed to support students who are reading these sections of the speech in preparation for OCR's AS Latin examination June 2015–June 2017. In these sections, Cicero concentrates on the suitability of Pompeius for an exceptional military command against Mithridates: the power of the speech derives from a skilful selection and arrangement of content, and from Cicero's masterful ability to build his rhetorical intensity to produce stirring and convincing conclusions. Understanding, therefore, of the speech rests upon an accurate translation of the Latin and a good sense of the political and ideological context within which the speech was written and delivered.

This edition contains a detailed introduction to the context of the speech, supported by a glossary of terms, timeline and a descriptive index of persons. The aim here is to help students find their way through a political and military set-up which is rather different (in both terminology and ideology) from our own. The notes to the speech itself aim to help students bridge the gap between GCSE and AS level Latin, and focus therefore on the harder points of grammar and word order, and on the structure and development of Cicero's argument. At the end of the book is a full vocabulary list for all the words contained in the prescribed sections.

At the end of the Introduction is an account of the key features of Cicero's rhetoric and style. It has been a deliberate decision, however, on the part of the editors not to give a word-by-word elucidation of these in the notes to accompany the Latin text. In part, this is because we hope that over the course of their study of this text, students will learn to engage with and identify Cicero's rhetorical techniques for themselves; but it is also because the choice of content for this speech should be the primary focus. Cicero's rhetoric supports his delivery of content, of course, but we did not wish the interest in the details and strands of his argument to be obscured by too single-minded a hunt for anaphora, exclamatio, homoioptoton, clausulae and so forth.

Katharine Radice wrote the notes and vocabulary, Catherine Steel the Introduction; we are very grateful to each other for incisive comments on various drafts. Our thanks are due to Stephen Anderson for his painstaking review of content, to Roger Rees for his thoughts on the Introduction, to OCR's anonymous reader for help with material on rhetorical figures and to Charlotte Loveridge and her team at Bloomsbury Academic.

Katharine Radice
Catherine Steel

Introduction

Setting the Scene

When Cicero delivered his speech *de imperio Cn. Pompei* (On the command of Gnaeus Pompeius) in 66 BC, he did so from the speakers' platform in the north-west corner of the Forum in Rome, close to the Senate House and with the slope of the Capitol rising up behind him. The speakers' platform – called the *rostra* (beaks), from the display on it of ships' prows, a trophy of the first war between Rome and Carthage almost two centuries earlier – was the normal location from which speakers addressed the Roman people, and since the second century BC, speakers on the *rostra* had faced outwards, across the Forum, in order to address as large an audience as possible. The Roman people as it gathered in this space was not, of course, remotely identical to all who held the Roman citizenship: by the first century BC, there were nearly half a million on the census list, of whom only a small proportion – some tens of thousands – could be simultaneously present in the Forum. The meeting at which Cicero spoke was a *contio*; the *contio* is sometimes described as an informal meeting, but it is perhaps best described as a 'briefing session': *contiones* did not have a formal decision-making role (though they could be held immediately before the people voted on a legislative proposal), but they could only be summoned by a magistrate or a tribune of the *plebs*, and the only people who could speak at a *contio* were those invited by the presiding magistrate or tribune so to do. Since the *contio* was not a voting assembly, there were, as far as we know, no restrictions on its listeners, and women and slaves might have been among Cicero's audience.

This *contio* had been summoned by one of the tribunes of the *plebs* in 66, C. Manilius, in order to tell the Roman people about a law he had put forward and on which they would soon be voting. As far as we can tell, Cicero was the only speaker (he does not refer to anyone who has spoken or is going to speak on this occasion), though Manilius will have introduced the meeting. Manilius' proposal – named, as was customary, after him, hence a *lex Manilia* – was to create a special military command against Mithridates VI, king of Pontus, and entrust it to Cn. Pompeius Magnus. To understand why and in what ways this was a controversial proposal, we need first to consider the nature of the Roman state and its geopolitical position, and then the careers and reputations of the individuals involved.

The Roman *Res Publica*

Rome was, by the mid-first century BC, a huge city by ancient standards, with a population of nearly a million, and the centre of an empire which was in control of most of the Mediterranean and the regions adjacent to it. Nonetheless, it retained the political organisation of a small city-state, in which adult male citizens were the ultimate arbiters through their capacity to declare war and pass laws: *res publica, res populi* ('the state is the people's possession') as Cicero put it a few years later in his treatise on government, *De re publica* (1.39). Executive authority was entrusted to annually elected magistrates, the most senior of which were the two consuls; the consuls, and their colleagues the eight praetors (a more junior position, which had to be held before the consulship) had *imperium*, the right to command, and consequently could lead Rome's armies. There was no distinction in Rome between senior military office and senior political office: the same men held both. In addition to the consuls and praetors, there were also four aediles each year (who were responsible for administration in the city of Rome) and 20 quaestors (who had a range of functions, largely financial). By the middle of the second century BC, a regular pattern of office-holding had emerged, the *cursus honorum*, which established the order quaestor–praetor–consul (the optional aedileship, if held, followed the quaestorship). Repeat office-holding was also banned, and this, combined with the principle of collegiality and the annual duration of magistracies, limited opportunities for individual members of the elite to consolidate personal power. The Roman Republic had its origins in the overthrow of monarchic rule at the end of the sixth century BC, and among the stories told of its early history were cautionary tales about men such as Spurius Maelius and Manlius Capitolinus who had aimed at individual power and consequently been brought down; such fears had been sharpened by the much more recent civil wars of the 80s BC, which had concluded with L. Cornelius Sulla's dictatorship in 82–79. Sulla had resigned his position and retired to private life, and the Republic had, to all appearances, resumed; but it still faced a real threat in the consolidation of individual power through military command.

Those who had held a magistracy became members of the Senate, which at this point was around 600 in size. In theory an advisory body for magistrates, the Senate had acquired a great deal of power of its own as Rome's empire expanded: its decrees, provided they were not vetoed, had long since acquired the force of law, and on a day-to-day basis it managed Rome's diplomatic activity, receiving embassies and adjudicating on disputes between allies. It also determined the military tasks to be entrusted to magistrates and the resources they would receive, a role which, in the light of the intricate nexus between military and political power at Rome, gave the Senate as a whole considerable power. Membership of the Senate was entirely confined to the wealthiest; candidates could not stand for election unless they possessed substantial property. In addition, men who were descended from families which had been active and successful in Roman political life for generations appear to have had an advantage in elections for the most senior magistracies; although the reasons for this are not fully understood, it may be connected with the structure of the voting assembly which elected consuls and praetors. Results were determined by voting units, not individual votes, and the wealthy voted in smaller units than the poor, giving their votes more weight in determining the outcome. Men without senatorial ancestry, such as Cicero, were at a considerable disadvantage in attempting to secure the consulship. Rome in the late Republic had no aristocracy, since no positions of power were hereditary; but it clearly had a ruling elite, which displayed considerable continuity from generation to generation. This elite could be described by the term *nobilitas*, 'nobility', and a man could be called *nobilis*, 'noble', if he were the descendant of a consul. The pressure on the *nobiles* to maintain their family's success over time was intense, and the strains were heightened by the influx of wealth to Rome following its conquest of the eastern Mediterranean in the second century BC, a windfall in which different senatorial families benefitted to differing degrees.

The power of the magistrates and Senate meant that Rome was not a democratic city-state in the way that, for example, Athens had been for most of the fifth and fourth centuries BC. Rome was not oligarchic, either; the power of the political elite was limited by elections, the need to obtain popular approval for legislation, and the principle of popular sovereignty. This principle was most clearly embodied in the ten annually-elected tribunes of the *plebs*. The office had its origins in the 'Struggle of the Orders' in the fifth and fourth centuries, when the plebeian majority of citizens attempted success-fully to obtain political equality with the patricians, a hereditary group who monopolised political office after the expulsion of the kings. The tribunate of the *plebs* was originally intended to protect individual plebeians from arbitrary punishment by patricians, and the authority of its holders was based on the oath which the plebeians had sworn to avenge themselves on anyone who harmed a tribune. As a result, tribunes possessed *sacrosanctitas*, sacrosanctity: they could not even be manhandled. As time passed, the tribunes acquired the right to propose legislation which was binding on the whole people, including patricians, and to veto decrees of the Senate and the acts of magistrates. By the first century BC, the plebeians had long had equal access to political office, and there were only a few patrician *gentes* (families) left, but the tribunate retained its powers and had become a way by which the people could challenge the patricio-plebeian *nobilitas* who formed the political elite. Not all tribunes asserted popular rights or challenged the nobility; many of its holders, indeed, were themselves *nobiles* and aspiring to follow the *cursus honorum* to higher office. But those who did use the tribunate to champion the rights and interests of the people were called *populares*.

Popularis politics had been an important element in Roman political life since the tribunate of Tiberius Gracchus in 133 BC, which had ended in his violent death, but had acquired particular potency in the years immediately prior to Manilius' law. In 82 BC, after a period of civil war, Sulla had captured Rome; during his dictatorship, which followed, he imposed radical changes to the *res publica*, including a huge increase in the size of the Senate and the end to tribunician legislative capacity. His intention was probably to reduce political violence; but his changes were, unsurprisingly, very unpopular, and as time passed, ambitious politicians sought to promote their own careers by repealing Sulla's measures. In 70, the consuls Pompeius and Crassus presided over the restoration of tribunes' right to propose laws, and over the following years there was a burst of *popularis* tribunician legislation, including this *lex Manilia*.

Rome and the Eastern Mediterranean

Rome had first sent an army east of the Adriatic in 229; its eastern ambitions were delayed by the long second war against Carthage, but almost immediately after that war came to an end, with Hannibal's defeat at Zama in 202, Rome attacked and defeated Philip V of Macedon and then turned its attention to the Hellenistic kingdoms east of the Aegean. Initially, Rome showed little interest in the annexation of territory, remaining content to exercise authority through and with local rulers. But in the late 130s BC, Attalus III of Pergamum died, leaving his kingdom to Rome. He almost certainly never intended this will to take effect; its purpose was rather to discourage assassination attempts. News of the bequest reached Rome during Tiberius Gracchus' tribunate, and at his instigation the people voted to use the profits which would be generated if the bequest were accepted to fund his proposals to redistribute land among poorer citizens. Enabling the Roman people to benefit directly from the profits of empire, rather than indirectly through the booty that made its way to soldiers and the various benefactions that commanders bestowed on Rome and its inhabitants, was entirely in keeping with the rest of Gracchus' radically *popularis* tenure of the tribunate, even if it was only a minor element in the opposition he faced which culminated in his death at the hands of a mob of senators led by the *Pontifex Maximus* (Chief Priest). Despite Gracchus' death, Roman armies were sent to Pergamum to take over the kingdom, which then became the Roman province of Asia. A few years later, Tiberius' brother Gaius, who was also a tribune of the *plebs* with a strongly *popularis* programme, arranged that the rights to gather taxes from Asia should be auctioned for a fixed fee which would come to the treasury. The bidders were groups of Roman equestrians (that is, men registered among the wealthiest property-holders at each census, but who had not sought elected office and membership of the Senate) and the successful groups then collected taxes directly from Asia; they were known as *publicani*, because they were dealing with a public contract. The *publicani* naturally wanted to gather as much revenue as possible, and managing the conflict of interest between them and local elites was a recurrent task for the Roman governors of Asia.

The initial annexation of Pergamum between 132 and 130 BC involved considerable fighting, but the province was then largely peaceful until Roman power in the region came into conflict with Mithridates VI, king of Pontus. Mithridates was born in the 130s BC and succeeded his father in 120; the Pontic kingdom at that point consisted of territory in northern Asia Minor. Mithridates pursued an ambitious and successful policy of expansion, allying himself with Armenia and absorbing smaller kingdoms in central Asia Minor; in 88 he responded to a Roman attack on Bithynia by invading Asia and killing as many Romans as he could find. Ancient sources give the number of dead as 80,000 which, even if exaggerated, points to the economic importance of Asia to Rome by this point and the scale of its exploitation.

Taking charge of a war against Mithridates was a very attractive opportunity for a Roman commander, because success would lead to great personal prestige as well as financial profit. The struggle to gain the command triggered civil war between different factions at Rome; in the end, Sulla, one of the consuls in 88 and the man to whom the Senate had initially entrusted the task, undertook the war, but his campaigning was overshadowed by events in Rome, and in order to return to Rome and secure his own position he concluded this First Mithridatic War in 84 BC, despite his victories in the battles of Chaeronea and Orchomenus, with a treaty on terms relatively favourable to Mithridates. (It was during this war, too, that Athens was sacked by the Romans.) One of the legates whom Sulla left behind engaged in further skirmishing, known as the Second Mithridatic War; but it was only in the mid-70s that the Romans decided seriously to resume the war and bring it to a successful conclusion.

The commander who was chosen on this occasion was L. Licinius Lucullus, an adherent of Sulla who held the consulship in 74 BC.

The Third Mithridatic War started very successfully for the Romans; Mithridates abandoned his kingdom and Lucullus advanced through Asia Minor to the headwaters of the Tigris and Euphrates, further east than Roman armies had ever previously gone. By 70, Lucullus seemed to have won the campaign, and he wrote to the Senate to announce his victory and ask for the despatch of ten commissioners to organise his conquests, and the following year he defeated Tigranes, king of Armenia and Mithridates' ally, at the Battle of Tigranocerta. Ancient accounts of the battle indicate an enormous disparity in the size of the two armies, with (according to Plutarch's *Lucullus*) 11,000 Romans facing 260,000 men in Tigranes' forces; and even if the actual figures need to be treated with some scepticism, this was clearly an extraordinary victory. But Lucullus' success was overall something of an illusion: Mithridates remained at large; Roman troops (some of whom had been in Asia since the First Mithridatic War) mutinied; and at Rome, Lucullus was attacked for prolonging the war in order to profit from it personally. In 67, Bithynia and the war against Mithridates were passed to the consul Manius Acilius Glabrio through a tribunician law, but Glabrio achieved little; in 66 the war still seemed to be a long way from conclusion.

The *Lex Manilia*

The war against Mithridates was, in 66, by far the longest-standing and most recalcitrant military problem which the Romans then faced. Whoever brought it to a successful conclusion would be extremely popular, and the tribune Manilius was attempting to harness this popularity through his law, which proposed putting Gnaeus Pompeius in charge of the war. This was not the only law that Manilius proposed; he began his year in office with a proposal to lift restrictions on voting by freedmen, which was passed but then annulled by the Senate on a technicality. His tribunate was very clearly *popularis*, and the *lex Manilia de imperio Cn. Pompei* was distinctly *popularis* in its approach. Although the people could perfectly well make decisions about foreign policy, it had become an area of policy which the Senate usually dealt with, and interventions in foreign affairs by tribunes of the *plebs* were inherently *popularis*. In addition, Gnaeus Pompeius, the beneficiary of Manilius' law, had a long and complex history in respect of the Senate and the people, and his explicit identification in the legislation also set up the potential for conflict between these two groups.

Pompeius

Gnaeus Pompeius was born on 29 September 106 into a family which contained senators and had produced its first consul in 141 BC. Pompeius' father, also called Gnaeus Pompeius, but with in addition the surname Strabo ('squinty'), was a senator at the time of his birth; he held the praetorship during the 90s BC, was a notably successful army commander during the Social War of 91–89 (when Rome's Italian allies, its *socii*, revolted and attempted, unsuccessfully, to establish a federal Italian state) and held the consulship in 89 BC. He took part in the civil war sparked by the struggle over the Mithridatic command, and he besieged Rome (possibly attempting to extort the right to stand for a second consulship), dying of disease during the siege. He was so unpopular that stories circulated that his death was due to lightning (suggesting divine hatred), and the younger Pompeius was prosecuted soon after on charges of being in possession of his father's illegally appropriated booty. Pompeius was acquitted, but it is reasonable to assume that he took to heart the importance of being popular with the Roman people; that is certainly an important motif throughout his career.

Pompeius became a protégé of Carbo, one of the dominant political figures during Sulla's absence from Rome, but late in 84 BC he changed sides, gathered and armed troops in Picenum where his family's estates were, and presented this force to Sulla when the latter returned with his army to Italy in the winter of 84–83 BC and resumed civil war against his enemies. His actions in so doing were illegal, since he had not been authorised by the Senate to raise an army, but Sulla regularised his position by bestowing *imperium* on him, although he had not held any elected office at Rome, let alone the praetorship or consulship. Irregularity remained the hallmark of Pompeius' career for the next decade. He pursued and defeated Sulla's opponents in Sicily and Africa (a period euphemistically described in paragraph 30 of *De Imperio Cn. Pompei*), and was rewarded with a triumph; it was at this point that his troops acclaimed him with the title Magnus, 'the Great'. He returned briefly to private life before receiving again a special grant of *imperium* in 77 to assist in suppressing an attempted coup which had been launched by one of the consuls of 78, M. Aemilius Lepidus. Once Lepidus had been defeated, Pompeius threatened to disobey the Senate's order that he should disband his forces; the crisis was defused only by sending Pompeius to Spain, to help in the fight against Sertorius, an ex-praetor who had escaped Sulla's advance and established a rival Roman authority in Spain. Sertorius was eventually assassinated by one of his own officers, and Pompeius and the other Roman commander, Metellus Pius, concluded the war by returning the Roman possessions in Spain to Rome's authority. Both men celebrated triumphs after their return to Rome, though in Pompeius' case this was only after a diversion, at the Senate's request, to assist in the final suppression of the slave revolt led by Spartacus. For Pius, his triumph was the culmination of a highly distinguished but nonetheless regular public career: he had held the consulship in 79 as one of Sulla's most trusted supporters. Pompeius, by contrast, was still not a member of the Senate; and whereas Pius was expected – as he did – to disband his army and resume the position of a distinguished senior member of the Senate, there was considerable anxiety about Pompeius' ambitions.

Pompeius' response to this potential crisis balanced exceptionalism against constitutional propriety: he indicated that he wanted to stand for the consulship. He had not held any of the necessary prior offices, and was also too young (the minimum age was 42); but the aspiration indicated that he intended to continue his career within the framework of the *res publica*. As a further sign that he was not a threat to established practice, he commissioned a handbook on senatorial procedure from his friend and former legate the polymath Varro (which, alas, does not survive). He also made it very clear that he intended, once elected, to restore the powers of the tribunate of the *plebs*; and he and his colleague as consul, M. Licinius Crassus, did so. Another important event in 70 was the election of censors. The census was normally carried out every five years, but had not been held since 86; in addition to registering citizens and revising the membership of the Senate, the censors performed the *lustrum*, a purification rite for the city and its citizens. When this took place at the end of the census in the summer of 69, Rome's inhabitants could feel that the violence and disruption of the recent civil wars and of Sulla's dictatorship were finally over; the incorporation of Pompeius peacefully into the Senate was an important element in that process of closure.

Pompeius chose not to take a province after his consulship; the normality of a proconsular command did not fit with his distinct profile. His opportunity to shine came soon, through the combination of the problem of piracy and the re-established powers of the tribunate. Piracy was endemic to the Mediterranean in antiquity: its suppression, which was only ever temporary, required a strong naval power. The island of Rhodes had controlled piracy effectively, but Rome ended its naval authority in the Aegean in the middle of the second century BC, and was slow to take on this role itself. In addition, the civil wars at Rome in the 80s BC had diverted resources. We can see the effects of this in Cicero's prosecution of Verres in 70 BC; one of the arguments in Verres' favour which Cicero needed to counter in his speeches was that Verres had campaigned successfully against pirate forces operating off Sicily. The Senate attempted to provide a concerted response in 74, when it established proconsular command against the pirates; but the man who held it – M. Antonius, the father of the triumvir – was defeated off Crete and died shortly afterwards. Crete was identified as a consular province again for one of the consuls of 69, Q. Caecilius Metellus, though he only reached his province in 68 and was dealing with only part of the problem. Piracy directly affected the inhabitants of Rome by driving up the price of food (much of the city's grain supply was imported by sea) and in 67 the tribune Gabinius put forward a proposal for a single, well-resourced command against the pirates whose holder would have *imperium* across the whole Mediterranean. His measure did not name the commander, simply specifying that it would be someone who had held the consulship; but Pompeius was clearly the intended recipient. The Senate was almost unanimously opposed to Gabinius' proposal, and many senators, including the former consuls Q. Lutatius Catulus and Q. Hortensius, spoke against it at *contiones*. Their opposition was perhaps influenced by the fact that the Senate's customary decision-making about foreign affairs was being usurped by the people directly; but Pompeius was the more serious issue. The structure and resources of the command itself were very similar to those which the Senate had given M. Antonius a few years earlier with which to deal with piracy; but that earlier command had caused no anxiety, presumably because the reputation and achievements of its holder were not exceptional. Equipping Pompeius, an exceptional tactician and fearsomely ambitious, with authority across the Mediterranean was, by contrast, a formidable prospect.

Gabinius' law was passed and Pompeius immediately began his campaign against the pirates. The most detailed evidence for his actions comes in fact from this speech, in which Cicero has every reason to emphasise Pompeius' brilliance; but, although Cicero in his speeches presents his case as well as he can, he does not, in general, make factually inaccurate statements and the overall account of Pompeius' campaigns that he gives in 34–35 can be accepted. Pompeius began in the western Mediterranean, moved his fleet eastward and within 50 days (Cicero puts the final victory *undequinquagesimo die*, 'on the forty-ninth day') defeated the pirates off the coast of Cilicia. He then turned his attention during the following winter to organisation, settling the pirates inland in Cilicia (he named one settlement Pompeiopolis, 'Pompeyville'). He also clashed with the commander in Crete, Metellus Creticus, over the handling of Cretan cities that were alleged to be involved in piracy. Pompeius may not have intended to acquire the Mithridatic command at the start of the pirate campaign, but by the winter of 67, he was close at hand to the relevant part of Rome's empire, he had ample forces at his disposal, and the generals to whom the war had been entrusted were a disappointment. We can be sure that he was in close contact with Rome and knew and approved of Manilius' measure. Co-operation between the two men gave Pompeius a further opportunity to display his military talents in solving a problem that had eluded others, and Manilius the chance to put forward a hugely popular measure. That popularity generated a broad spectrum of support among the elite for the *lex Manilia*, unlike the previous year's *lex Gabinia*. Among those who now decided that support for Pompeius' exceptional *imperium* was desirable was one of the year's praetors, M. Tullius Cicero.

Cicero

Cicero was born on 3 January 106 at Arpinum, a town about 60 miles east of Rome (modern Arpino). Arpinum had received Roman citizenship in 188 BC; the first man from Arpinum to play a prominent role in the political life of Rome was Gaius Marius, who reached the consulship in 107, and by defeating the Celtic tribes, which, at the end of the second century, threatened northern Italy, he became, for a while, Rome's greatest living hero and the holder of unprecedented repeated consulships. At the end of his life his desire for the command against Mithridates triggered the civil war with Sulla. The Tullii were linked to Marius' family through marriage, and they and a third family, the Gratidii, dominated Arpinum, good examples of the so-called *domi nobiles* ('nobles in their own communities'), the wealthy local elites who ran affairs in Italian towns. *Domi nobiles* often had links with prominent men at Rome, and their votes were important in elections at Rome; but neither Cicero's grandfather nor father attempted to stand for office at Rome or enter the Senate, unlike Marius. However, Cicero's father moved his family to Rome during the 90s BC, and Cicero and his younger brother Quintus studied rhetoric and oratory there. Cicero also spent time with members of the Senate with whom his father had connections, including the augur and former consul Q. Mucius Scaevola, and the leading orators of the day, L. Licinius Crassus and M. Antonius (the grandfather of Julius Caesar's lieutenant and the lover of Cleopatra, whose name, also M. Antonius, is commonly anglicised as Mark Antony). Cicero provided a glimpse of this world in the settings of some of the philosophical and rhetorical treatises which he wrote in the 50s and 40s BC, particularly *De oratore*, which purports to report a conversation about oratory and orators between Crassus, Antonius and a group of their friends in September 91 BC.

The setting of *De oratore* was intentionally poignant: Crassus died only a few days later, and in the following weeks Rome was engulfed in crisis, as its Italian allies revolted and the Social War began. Cicero's formal transition to adulthood may have taken place in March 90, at the festival of the *Liberalia*; soon afterwards he began his military service. Interestingly, the elder Cicero chose to place his son as a trainee not in the army of his fellow-Arpinate Marius, but in that of Pompeius Strabo (the father of Pompeius Magnus); it is possible that Marius' sympathies with *popularis* politics caused tensions between the two families. Cicero says very little about his experiences during the Social War in his writings (a couple of unrevealing anecdotes are recalled in his late philosophical works), but it seems reasonable to assume that he did not find military life congenial; certainly, as soon as the war was over he left the army. During the 80s BC he remained in Rome, studying oratory and philosophy and, as he recalls in his history of Roman oratory, *Brutus* (section 308), listening to speakers. The dominant political figures at Rome were L. Cornelius Cinna and Cn. Papirius Carbo; they were opponents of Sulla and it was evident that there would be war once Sulla returned from the campaign against Mithridates. That war lasted for two years (84–82), ending with Sulla's victory and the extensive revenge that he took on his enemies through the proscriptions (the publication of the names of his opponents, who thereupon could be killed with impunity; their property was confiscated). Marius' son (also called Gaius Marius) and his adopted son Marius Gratidianus fought against Sulla and both were killed during the war; the Tullii remained neutral and escaped with lives and property unscathed.

Cicero made his oratorical debut in 81 with a speech, *Pro Quinctio*, in a civil law case, a dispute about property between business partners; the opposing side's lawyer was Hortensius, who had emerged as the leading orator of the post-Social War generation. Cicero's client probably lost his case (it seems unlikely that Cicero would nowhere have recorded an early victory over Hortensius, had he been successful); nonetheless, Cicero thought his speech worth recording and disseminating. Roman orators had long been preserving their speeches in written form – the elder Cato, who was active in the first half of the second century BC, was a particularly prolific example – but to do so remained a choice. Antonius, for example, never did so, on the grounds that if he did so he could be caught out in self-contradiction (Cic. *Pro Cluentio* section 140). Others recorded only a few speeches. It was therefore an act of noticeable ambition for a novice orator, with few connections among the Roman elite, to preserve a speech in a legal case which had little if any wider significance or interest to those not directly involved. Dissemination of *Pro Quinctio* should be set alongside Cicero's earlier work on rhetoric, *De inventione*, which he wrote during the 80s. Although *De inventione* is incomplete (it covers only the first of the five processes involved in writing a speech according to ancient rhetorical theory) and derivative (its content is very similar to the anonymous *Rhetorica ad Herennium*, written at around the same time: both authors probably attended lectures by the same teacher), it does contain in its preface an ambitious statement of the importance of rhetoric to civil society; and the very act of Cicero's arranging for it to be copied and distributed suggests that he was thinking about his reputation and the ways in which it could be enhanced by a textual presence even before he made his oratorical début. (Cicero, like almost all authors in antiquity, self-published; he arranged for a few copies to be made, probably by his own literate slaves, and sent them to his friends and those to whom he wished to advertise his achievements. With no copyright, it was then open to anyone who came across a copy to make one for his own use; copies of Cicero's speeches and other works multiplied, and thus survived to the invention of printing, because of his fame and his works' use as school-texts.)

Cicero's next case was far more important than Quinctius' property dispute; it involved alleged parricide (the murder of a parent) and was also tangled up in Sulla's proscriptions. His client was Sextus Roscius, the son of a wealthy land-owner from Ameria, a town about 50 miles up the Tiber valley from Rome. The elder Roscius had died violently, and his son was accused of having arranged the murder (he died in Rome, when his son was in Ameria). The case was complicated by the elder Roscius' name having appeared on the proscription list, and his death should therefore have been exempted from any legal penalty against the perpetrator. Cicero does not, however, use that argument; instead, he claims that the men who brought the prosecution (relatives of Roscius) were also responsible for the post-mortem addition of the elder Roscius' name to the proscription list in order to acquire his property at a bargain price. This narrative was risky insofar as it suggested that Sulla's regime was corrupt; Cicero tried to neutralise that danger by claiming that the person who added Roscius' name was one of Sulla's freedmen, L. Cornelius Chrysogonus, and that Sulla himself knew nothing of the affair. It is not really clear why Cicero chose this line of defence, rather than the much more straightforward argument based on the proscription list (though it succeeded; Roscius was acquitted); it may well have been that Roscius refused to be portrayed as his father's murderer, whatever the circumstances or dangers, and the strategy may also have seemed to offer a better prospect of getting his property back from the prosecutors. Its consequences for Cicero himself are also debated. Cicero left Rome shortly afterwards for an extended tour of the eastern Mediterranean, during which he spent time at Athens and on Rhodes; and it has been argued that he did so because he was afraid of Sulla's retribution. Cicero himself in a later work explained his departure on the grounds of weak health and poor speaking technique (*Brutus* sections 313–14) which he wished to improve through further study. Moreover, *Pro Sexto Roscio*

Amerino is careful to minimize offence to Sulla by restricting blame to a relatively unimportant member of his entourage; and it could be argued that the speech's emphasis on moving on from a period of lawlessness to the re-establishment of order under the benevolent leadership of the *nobilitas* fitted with Sulla's own aims and vision for the *res publica*.

Once Cicero returned to Rome he began his political career by standing for the quaestorship, to which he was elected for the year 75 BC; he served in Sicily, based at Lilybaeum (Marsala). Years later he wryly recalled his return to Rome at the end of his year's service (*Pro Plancio* sections 64–66), describing how he assumed that everyone was talking about his success there, only to find, when he reached the seaside resort of Puteoli, that he was taken for a visitor from Rome and no one knew anything about him; 'I realised that the Roman people were rather deaf, but had excellent eyesight.' From that time, he says, he concentrated on being well known in the city. For Cicero, that meant oratory; he had a number of cases in the latter part of the 70s, but none as striking or successful as the defence of Roscius, which may have contributed to the gamble he took in 70, when he launched a prosecution for extortion against Gaius Verres, the former governor of Sicily who was planning to stand for the consulship. There was no centralised prosecution service in Rome; prosecutors were private individuals, and so the act of prosecution was always liable to seem to be an act of personal hostility (though prosecutors could also use arguments about the safety of the *res publica*, as Cicero does against Verres). If Verres had been acquitted, Cicero would have acquired an unpleasant enemy; but, through meticulous preparation and, following the election of Pompeius and Crassus as consuls, in a political climate favourable to reform, Cicero secured Verres' conviction, and Verres went into exile at Massilia. Both politically and oratorically, Cicero's career now proceeded without a hitch. He defended his first senatorial client the following year (the ex-praetor

Fonteius, on extortion charges; the surviving fragments of his speech show Cicero defending Fonteius for actions not dissimilar to those he had attacked in Verres) and in the summer of 67 was elected at the head of the poll to the position of praetor for 66. This was the position he held when he spoke in favour of the Manilian law on Pompeius' command. Cicero's aim in delivering this speech was not simply to secure the people's approval for Manilius' proposal. Indeed, his contribution to the law's passage was probably negligible: given Pompeius' popularity and the level of public trust in his military abilities, Manilius' law passed with very little opposition. Cicero contributed to the debate for his own benefit. It allowed him to demonstrate his popular credentials; and, unlike the previous year's *lex Gabinia*, support for Manilius' measure did not involve taking a position in opposition to many of the Senate's senior members. It offered the perfect opportunity for a safe *popularis* display.

The Speech

Rhetorical theory divided oratory into three basic categories: forensic, that is speeches delivered in legal cases; deliberative (political speeches); and epideictic ('display' speeches, which praised or blamed individuals: these included funeral speeches and, in the imperial period, speeches praising the emperor, such as the younger Pliny's *Panegyricus*). *De imperio Cn. Pompei* is a deliberative speech, and as such it is fundamentally an answer to the question, 'What should we do?' Rhetorical instruction devoted the greatest level of detail to forensic oratory, and the much briefer advice it offered for deliberative speeches assumed only two fundamental arguments in favour of a course of action: that it was honourable, or that it was materially advantageous. Ideally, both should be used in tandem; difficulties arose when the two criteria pointed in different directions. Cicero claims that entrusting the command against Mithridates to Pompeius is both honourable and advantageous. It is honourable because Rome's military *gloria* (glory) is involved (11–12) and its obligations to its allies demand action (12–13); it is an advantageous course of action because it will protect Rome's revenues (14–16) and the position of the *publicani*, on whose prosperity effective tax-collection depends (17–19).

These considerations about honour and advantage take up the first section of the argument (*argumentatio*), which begins at 6; it is preceded by the *exordium*, introduction (1–3) and the *narratio*, statement of facts (4–5). In many speeches, particularly forensic ones, the *narratio* is extensive because the audience needs to know a complex set of facts; here, the *narratio* is short because Cicero assumes that everyone is aware of the war against Mithridates. That was presumably a reasonable assumption in Rome in 66 BC, but as we shall see, the simplicity of the *narratio* also contributes to Cicero's overall strategy. Cicero begins his *argumentatio* by identifying three topics he will discuss. The first is the nature of the war (*genus belli*), in which Cicero employs the conventional deliberative arguments discussed above; he then (20–26) moves to its size, *magnitudo*, to demonstrate its danger; finally (27–48), he moves to the choice of commander, *de imperatore deligendo*. But he immediately explains that Pompeius is the only man fit for the task: 'what grounds are there to cause anyone to doubt this?' The third section thus becomes an analysis of Pompeius' brilliance as a leader. The *argumentatio* concludes with a summary of its content (49–50) and Cicero then counters the arguments put forward by opponents of Manilius' law (*refutatio*, 51–67) before listing the law's supporters (68) and concluding with renewed encouragement to the audience to vote in favour combined with a promise that he will always work on their behalf (69–71).

In comparison with many of Cicero's speeches, the structure of *de imperio Cn. Pompei* is easy to identify and analyse, with clearly marked divisions between sections and detailed guidance from Cicero as to what he is about to cover. The simplicity of structure may be connected with the nature of the audience, whose members were not necessarily oratorically trained (unlike the jurors in forensic cases at Rome, who all were wealthy individuals who were likely to have studied rhetoric and in addition heard several cases each year). This was also the first occasion on which Cicero had addressed the Roman people, and he may as a result have chosen a straightforward approach. But simplicity also helps Cicero's argument, because he claims that this is a simple case, in which the right course of action is obvious. Hence the brief *narratio*, which gives the impression that there is nothing in dispute about the situation. The argument itself unfolds inexorably, as though in answer to a sequence of questions. Why do we need to do something? (Because our interests, material and ethical, are threatened.) Why do we need to act now? (Because the threat is serious.) Why choose Pompeius to take action? (Because he is outstanding in every respect.) However, when the argument is laid out in this form, it is possible to see that a question is missing, namely, why address the threat in this way? That is, Cicero ignores in his argument the controversial aspect of Manilius' proposal, namely to remove the war against Mithridates from the normal process of military planning involving the oversight of the Senate and annually-elected magistrates and to respond to it instead via the creation of a special command with exceptionally extensive powers. Not only did this aspect of the law place it firmly in the *popularis* tradition of challenge to senatorial authority; it also consolidated the power of Pompeius, whose position within the *res publica* was already anomalously prominent.

It is only in the *refutatio* that Cicero turns to the opponents of the law, and even there he may well have simplified their case (we depend on Cicero's speech to know what Catulus and Hortensius said). Hortensius' position is characterised as opposition to the idea of a single commander (52–58). Cicero responds with an argument from analogy, reminding the audience that Hortensius spoke against the *lex Gabinia*: Hortensius was wrong then, and is wrong now. The approach also gives Cicero the opportunity to retell the story of Pompeius' success against the pirates. Catulus' reported objection is based on potential vulnerability: if the people place all their hope in Pompeius, what would be the result if anything were to happen to Pompeius? It seems unlikely that that was Catulus' only hesitation about the *lex Manilia*, but it does give Cicero the opportunity to tell an anecdote which shows Catulus in a favourable light: Catulus put his question to the Roman people, and they responded by saying that in those circumstances, they would turn to Catulus himself. Cicero concludes his response to Catulus with a brief account of innovation in Roman military practice and the innovations that have already taken place in Pompeius' case. Cicero thus neutralises the force of the objections to the law without engaging in the substantive issues, whilst creating further opportunities to record and retell Pompeius' achievements.

The praise of Pompeius in sections 27–48 is arranged under four headings: military knowledge, *scientia rei militaris*; virtue, *virtus*; prestige, *auctoritas*; and luck, *felicitas*. Cicero's approach initially is to demonstrate that Pompeius possesses these qualities by narrating his actions, a tactic which involves some repetition: Cicero covers Pompeius' achievements prior to his consulship in both *scientia* (28) and *virtus* (29–35) and in each of the first three sections the campaign against the pirates is cited. Variety is maintained by its increasing prominence: in *scientia*, it is referred to simply as a *bellum navale*, naval war, in a list which demonstrates the range of Pompeius' experience of different kinds of campaign from the very start of his career; in *virtus*, there is a long account (31–35) which concentrates on the size of the war and the decisive nature of Pompeius' victory. Cicero then expands his focus, from *virtus* as courage to *virtus* as virtue (a slippage already well-established in Latin usage by this period) to include a range of Pompeius' qualities, including self-control, integrity and intelligence, all of which are exemplified from his conduct during the pirate war. Finally, his *auctoritas* is also shown in this war, partly through the Roman people's demand that he should take charge of the campaign and partly through the effect that Pompeius' reputation has already had (Cicero claims) in slowing the progress of Mithridates' campaign. Cicero uses the first three headings to ram home the message that Pompeius has been responsible for a recent major success, in an issue which directly affected the well-being of his listeners. The final quality, good luck, *felicitas*, is handled in a rather different way. Cicero begins this section by acknowledging that luck is in the control of the gods, and no man can claim it for his own; but it is possible to recognise it in others. He does not choose to detail Pompeius' achievements yet again, confining himself to remarking on the sheer scale of Pompeius' good fortune and to linking it to the 'shared safety and command' of all his listeners.

Each of these four characteristics was clearly a good quality for a military leader to possess as well as being valued in Roman culture. It is possible that Cicero was also influenced by Hellenistic treatises on kingship, the genre which appears to have been popular in the third and second centuries BC, though examples do not survive, and which identified a range of characteristics which rulers should ideally possess. If there are links, however, the significance lies less in the details than in the fact of Pompeius being described in terms which recall kingship, given the hostility in Republican Roman culture, at least on the part of the political elite, to monarchic rule. But we do not need to invoke such possible models in order to identify what is so striking about Cicero's approach. The praise of Pompeius works in complete harmony with the basic premise of Manilius' law, that military commands should be allocated on the basis of talent and performance. This seems to us such an eminently sensible position that it is easy to underestimate the challenge it posed to the norms of Republican government, which had developed over centuries precisely in order to control competition between members of the elite and, by restricting the link between talent and reward, to prevent the emergence of powerful individuals with potential tyrannical ambitions.

There is nothing comparable to Cicero's praise of Pompeius in earlier Latin literature, and its force and brilliance were largely responsible for the speech as a whole becoming a model to later writers and being preserved through late antiquity and into the medieval period. Although the speech is, in formal terms, deliberative, the praise of Pompeius could be read as a piece of epideictic oratory and, as such, it offered an example to imperial speakers in their addresses to emperors. Indeed, Fronto (the Emperor Marcus Aurelius' tutor) sent a copy to the Emperor Verus when the latter was campaigning against the Parthians in the 160s AD, saying 'no-one ever seems to me to have been praised at a public meeting, whether in Greek or Latin, more eloquently than Gnaeus Pompeius is praised in this speech – so he seems to acquire the surname "Great" through Cicero's praises, not his own qualities. In it you will find many sections well fitted to your current deliberations ...' (*De Bello Parthico* 10). It is a paradox, and one that Cicero would not have enjoyed, that two of his most widely-read speeches – this one, with its praise of Pompeius, and *Pro Marcello*, from 46 BC, which praises the dictator Caesar – were popular precisely because they showed how to praise a single powerful figure in terms incompatible with the republican constitution to which Cicero was so deeply committed.

It is also possible to identify some specific issues about Pompeius' career prior to 66 which affected Cicero's description of it. The strong focus on the pirate campaign, rather than the period before Pompeius' consulship, makes sense, as discussed above, because it was recent and relevant; but Pompeius had triumphed twice before he became consul, so there was a great deal that could have been celebrated about the earlier period. On the other hand, his early experience took place during the civil war between Sulla and his opponents; and he had been responsible for the deaths of a large number of distinguished Romans. A very different story about Pompeius *could* be told; and we get a glimpse of what that might look like in a fragment of a speech from 55 BC (Valerius Maximus book 6, section 2.8), in which Pompeius' early acts are listed and attacked and the speaker concludes by describing him as an *adulescentulus carnifex*, a 'teenage butcher'.

Cicero's speech derives most of its persuasive force from the attractiveness of Pompeius and the genuine scale of his career, but it relies as well on a particular construction of Roman imperialism. In 66 BC, Roman power in the Mediterranean was in a process of transition from an empire based on the giving of orders to one based on territorial control. That is, as Rome first conquered the Hellenistic kingdoms in the second century BC, it exerted its power through orders given to local rulers and communities; provided those orders were obeyed, Rome did not interfere further. As time passed, however, more direct control was imposed: this can be seen, for example, in tax-collection, which, from the 120s BC in Asia and subsequently elsewhere, was in the hands of Romans. One consequence of this development was a predictable flow of income to the Roman treasury; and a regular strand in *popularis* politics was the demand that the *commoda*, benefits, of empire be shared among the citizen body as a whole. The preferred method was the provision of subsidised (and, later, free) wheat, which was begun by Gaius Gracchus in 123 BC and continued, with a brief suspension by Sulla, for the rest of the Republican period and well beyond. When Cicero describes Mithridates' threat to his audience's *vectigalia*, 'taxes' (4–8), and claims that their loss threatens the *pacis ornamenta* (6), 'ornaments of peace', he is, discreetly, aligning himself with this approach. He also does so in his emphasis on Pompeius' probity in sections 37–42. The alternative to public exploitation of empire was private benefit: military commanders had considerable opportunities, more or less legal, to enrich themselves (reflected in the legislation on extortion, *res repetundae*), and suspicions that Lucullus was behaving in this way was one of the factors in his recall. By emphasising that Pompeius does not take money for himself, Cicero is rounding out his characterisation of Pompeius as the ideal commander.

The *popularis* colouring to Cicero's handling of Roman imperialism gives an important clue to his self-presentation in this speech: as he prepared to launch the following year his campaign for the consulship, it was vitally important – particularly given his status as a new man – to acquire popular support. But we should note how carefully Cicero does so: he did not wish to alienate the wealthy by suggesting radicalism. Cicero begins the speech by explaining that he has never before addressed the people at a *contio*. He explains that he did not wish to do so until his talent was adequate, and that he had been occupied in serving his friends (that is, acting as a defence advocate). Lurking here is the fact that Cicero had chosen not to be a tribune of the *plebs*, an office which was open to him but which would, in the late 70s, have involved him in the struggles over repeal of aspects of Sulla's changes. The careful appeal to all audiences can also be seen in the politeness with which he treats Lucullus, Catulus and Hortensius. Lucullus' reverses were due to *fortuna*, chance (10) – 'L. Lucullus left the war after great achievements' (5) – and his campaigning receives a laudatory summary in 20–21. The audience is left in no doubt that he failed, but there is no invective or blame. Catulus and Hortensius, similarly, are treated in the most honorific fashion. These three men were among the most senior and influential members of the Senate; Cicero did not wish to alienate them. In the *De imperio* speech we can see his attempt to build a broad consensus, a policy he was to follow, with the occasional deviation, throughout his political career.

Subsequent Events

Manilius was prosecuted on extortion charges as soon as he had left office as tribune on 9 December 66; this court was presided over in 66 by Cicero, who postponed the hearing into the following year (when one of the new praetors would take over) and this case petered out, but Manilius was convicted in 65 on treason charges arising from his conduct as tribune. Gabinius, by contrast, prospered; he took a position on Pompeius' staff during the war against Mithridates, stood successfully for the praetorship after his return and was consul in 58 BC. His proconsular command was in Syria; he was convicted after his return to Rome on extortion charges, recalled from exile by Caesar, and died of illness in 47 whilst fighting for Caesar during the civil war.

Pompeius began his campaign against Mithridates and Mithridates' ally (and son-in-law) Tigranes as soon as the *lex Manilia* was passed. He, like Lucullus, found it difficult to secure a decisive victory over Mithridates. Instead, he concentrated his efforts against the Hellenistic kingdom of Syria, which was in a desperately chaotic state, and Judaea, where a civil war was raging. Syria was annexed, and – after entering the sanctuary of the Temple in Jerusalem – Pompeius installed a pro-Roman faction in Judaea. During the siege of Jerusalem in the autumn of 63, Pompeius' famed luck came to his assistance; news arrived that Mithridates was dead, having committed suicide when faced with an uprising by his son Pharnaces. Pompeius began a slow and triumphant return to Italy via Asia Minor (where he received Mithridates' embalmed body) and Greece, reaching Brundisium in the winter of 62–61. He faced great difficulties in getting senatorial ratification for his organisation of the territories he had conquered, as a result of which he formed an alliance with Caesar in 60. Caesar, as consul in 59, delivered ratification; but the suspension of normal political processes that year severely dented Pompeius' popularity, and he relied on the support of Caesar's soldiers to secure re-election to the consulship in 55 (again with Crassus as colleague). He held a third consulship in 52 in response to the crisis caused by the murder of the *popularis*, and very popular, politician Publius Clodius; he restored order successfully, but this achievement was overshadowed by the breakdown of trust between Caesar and the Senate over the procedure to bring Caesar's Gallic campaign to an end, which led to the outbreak of civil war in January 49 BC. Pompeius was appointed chief commander of the senatorial forces and was defeated by Caesar at Pharsalus in 48 BC; he escaped to Egypt, hoping to rebuild his position there, but was killed by the Egyptians as he arrived to prevent their becoming embroiled in a Roman civil war.

Cicero was elected to the consulship for 63; as consul, he exposed an attempted coup organised by a disaffected noble, Catiline, and his actions in suppressing it had profound effects on the rest of his career. On the instruction of the Senate, he had five of Catiline's associates executed; an army led by the other consul, C. Antonius (son of Antonius the orator), defeated Catiline's forces early in 62. The legality of the executions, which had taken place without any judicial process, was dubious; and Cicero was exiled on those grounds in 58 BC through a law proposed by Clodius, who held the tribunate in this year. (Cicero and Clodius had been personal enemies since Cicero gave evidence against Clodius when he was being tried for sacrilege in 61 and this was probably an element in Clodius' campaign against Cicero, though the right to a trial was a central plank in *popularis* thinking.) He was recalled from exile in 57 due largely to support from Pompeius and Caesar, but found his independence severely compromised thereafter; after a great deal of hesitation, he chose the senatorial side in the civil war and was eventually pardoned by Caesar. During Caesar's dictatorship he wrote the great series of philosophical works on which his reputation in late antiquity and the medieval period so heavily depended; after Caesar was assassinated in 44 BC he emerged from retirement to challenge Marcus Antonius' quest for monarchical power through the *Philippics*. The attempt ended in failure when Antonius established an alliance with Caesar's great-nephew and heir Octavian and with Marcus Lepidus; the three men revived Sulla's device of proscription, and Cicero's name was on their list. He was killed in December 43 BC.

Language and Style

Oral interaction between members of the elite and the Roman people was a very important aspect of political life at Rome; unsurprisingly, Roman politicians were keen to speak persuasively. Rhetorical education began in adolescence and was based on declamation, the composition and delivery of practice speeches; students worked on both forensic (*controversiae*) and deliberative (*suasoriae*) oratory. Collections of declamations survive from the imperial period, and give an idea of the kinds of material which students might have handled; the scenarios are frequently fantastical, involving improbable coincidences and stock characters, but were intended to make students think about how to build a convincing argument and practise using language appropriately. Such exercises were supplemented by practical experience; young men who aspired towards public life would accompany politicians in their day-to-day activities, the so-called *tirocinium fori*, 'forum training'.

The use of language – *elocutio* – was, according to ancient rhetorical theory, a distinct part of the process of composing a speech. After a speaker had identified the arguments he would use (*inventio*) and decided on the most effective order in which to present them (*dispositio*), he would decide on the appropriate style and put his arguments into words. The final parts of the process involved preparing the performance of the speech in terms of gestures and tone of voice (*actio*) and, since ancient orators spoke without a script, committing the whole edifice to memory (*memoria*). *Elocutio* began with decisions about the overall style of the speech. Three fundamental styles were identifed, 'simple', 'middle' and 'grand', which were distinguished by their degree of syntactical complexity but also by their increasing emotional charge. In addition, the different styles became linked to what were called the *officia oratoris*, the orator's duties: to teach (*docere*), to please (*delectare*) and to move (*movere*). A simple style was appropriate to instruction (as, for example, in the *narratio* of a speech); the middle style gave pleasure; and the high style was to be used when the audience's emotions were to be stirred up. The *Rhetorica ad Herennium* (4.11–16) discusses the three styles with illuminating examples, including ones showing how each style could go wrong. Cicero himself was too experienced a speaker by 66 BC to be bound rigidly by rhetorical handbooks, but it is clear nonetheless that *De imperio* is in the middle style: Cicero is conciliatory towards his audience, and the matter itself is sufficiently important to demand something more than the simplest style, but there is no need of high emotion (as there was in his defence speeches, where his client's very existence as a Roman citizen was often at stake).

One aspect of *elocutio* was the use of rhetorical figures. This aspect of rhetoric was elaborated in enormous detail by writers on rhetoric (perhaps because it lends itself to the creation of lists; books 8–9 of Quintilian's *Institutio Oratoriae* offer a comprehensive treatment, with many citations from earlier Latin literature). However, the importance of rhetorical figures in making language effective and persuasive can be overestimated: the *De imperio Cn. Pompei*, as one would expect in a speech which generally eschews passage of strong emotion, contains relatively few rhetorical figures, and relies instead on lucid argumentation, Pompeius' popularity, and Cicero's presentation of himself as a reasonable and sympathetic character. To use the terms of Aristotle's tripartite analysis in his *Rhetoric* (which Cicero adopted in *De oratore*), it relies on *logos* (argument) and *ethos* (character) to a greater extent than it does on *pathos* (emotion). Nonetheless, an understanding of rhetorical figures is important in grasping the effectiveness of Cicero's style in the *De imperio*, and those sitting the examination for which this edition is published will need to be aware of, and show their grasp of, these features. In discussing style, it is the *aim* and *effect* of the stylistic feature that need to be grasped, rather than the technical terms. That is why, as the preface to this edition makes clear, detailed discussion of the style points has been consciously avoided in the commentary; it is speaking, hearing and discussing the points when reading them in the text that prove most useful in helping to appreciate Cicero's skill. But the technical terms are given in the discussion below, not least because they are the ones used in ancient rhetorical textbooks and in modern treatments of the topic.

The list below identifies the most important figures of speech to be found in this speech; it is no coincidence that Cicero favours figures, such as anaphora, which help him to create balanced sentences which, even if they are long, develop in a logical and comprehensible fashion. The *De imperio* needed to be understood on a single hearing, and that is Cicero's guiding stylistic principle.

- 'Rhetorical' questions are found widely through the prescribed sections. Cicero often asks his audience questions to which the answer is obvious – usually either 'no one' or 'Pompeius'. The posing of a question is intended to prompt the listener to think for himself and so more fully and directly involve the listener in grasping the point being made.

- Stylistic repetition of the same word at the beginning of a number of clauses or sentences which closely follow one another is known as 'anaphora'. It is a heavily used technique for emphasis in the prescribed sections of the speech: see for instance section 28 (where *qui* is repeated); section 30 (*testis*); section 36 (*quantae – quanta – quanto*); and section 41 (*nunc*).

- Cicero will at times omit connecting words, as in section 34, *Siciliam adiit, Africam exploravit*; or section 35, *extrema hieme apparavit, ineunte vere suscepit, media aestate confecit*. This is called 'asyndeton', and often gives the points being made a certain rapidity or clarity of focus.

- 'Chiasmus' is the reversal of the word order in the second half of a pair of expressions or statements, which gives the whole phrase or sentence a feeling of emphasis, e.g. in section 30, *testis est Sicilia, quam multis undique cinctam periculis **non terrore belli, sed consilii celeritate** explicavit*; and section 31, *aut ab omnibus imperatoribus uno anno, aut omnibus annis ab uno imperatore*.

- The example from section 35 is also an example of the use of three statements or expressions, in which the second has more weight than the first and the third more weight still (*apparavit, suscepit, confecit*). This common rhetorical device is known as the 'tricolon crescendo' (or 'tricolon crescens' or 'tricolon auctum'). Cicero is skilled enough to use more than one style point at the same time.

- There is at times some direct and emotional exclamation to the audience, for instance in section 27 (*utinam ... putaretis!*). This can be called 'exclamatio'.

- When Cicero finds he can use repetition of case endings in the same position in one clause or sentence after another, he is using a rhetorical or stylistic device known as 'homoioptoton'. An example comes from section 27, *genere ipso necessarium, magnitudine periculosum.* This gives a potentially memorable neatness to the phrasing.

- If there is a series of phrases or clauses of similar length and structure, as in sections 28 (*non ... sed ...*) or 29 (*labor in negotiis ... consilium in providendo*), this is a point of rhetorical style known as 'isocolon'. This can be used either to point up the similarity between points, and so give them, and the connection between them, extra emphasis, or do the same for any difference or contrast between them.

- In section 32 (*cum duodecim secures in praedonum potestatem pervenerint*), Cicero is not only perhaps emphasising his point with the repetition of the 'p' sound – and repetition of consonants is known as alliteration – but he is also employing a style point known as 'metonymy'. This is where a part of something is mentioned as standing for the whole. The *secures* (axes) stand for the magistrates' attendants, or *lictors*, who carried them as a symbol of the magistrates' authority. *Praetors* were assigned six lictors when outside the city of Rome, and Cicero is referring here to the two praetors who were captured by pirates, and the insult to their authority this implies is emphasised also by the mention of the axes.

- The use of more words than is necessary is a favourite device of Cicero. For example, look at *attenuatum atque imminutum* or *sublatum ac sepultum* in section 30. This device is called 'pleonasm'; it adds emphasis and importance to the moment being described or the point being made, and it may not be simply ornamental. Cicero has only one chance to persuade his audience, and they only one chance to hear, so this extra doubling of the point at issue by 'repetition' of similar words has a clear reason behind it.

- Another form of rhetorically useful repetition is that of a word in a different grammatical form, for instance *veneant atque venierint* in section 37. The technical term for this is 'polyptoton'.

- Cicero also tends to mark off the movement from one point of argument or persuasion to another by the style technique called 'transitio' (a transitional statement). An example comes in section 27 *satis mihi .. videatur.*
- It is also wise to look out for:
  - deliberate use of superlative adjectives or adverbs, especially where more than one is used close together;
  - the conscious alteration of what might be thought of as natural or normal word order by putting a key word or phrase in the most emphatic places at the beginnings or ends of phrases, clauses or sentences or even before that part of the sentence to which they really belong, as a lead into the point being made.

One other aspect of Cicero's oratorical style should be mentioned: his use of clausulae, that is, of particular rhythmical patterns to mark the end of a clause or sentence. Clausulae were particularly useful in an oral performance context, since they indicated for the audience where there was a pause; in his later treatise *Orator*, which deals with prose rhythm, Cicero remarks on the applause which met a speaker's skilful use of a clausula in a speech at a *contio* (*Orator* 213–14).

These rhythmic patterns are based on length of syllable (which is determined in exactly the same way as in Latin verse); the commonest clausulae which Cicero uses include (in each case the final syllable can be either short or long):

–u– –u (and its variant –uuu –u); for example, 27, *esse videatur*; 33, *esse sublatos*; 36, *imperatoris*

–u– –u– (and its variant – – – –u–); for example, 32, *summa transmiserint*; 42, *victi dilexerint*

–u– –u–u (and its variants –uu– –u–u and – –u– u–u–); for example, 29, *audivimus, non fuerunt*; 31, *omnes sinus atque portus.*

Avoidance of the rhythm of the ending of a hexameter line was another important principle of Cicero's oratorical prose rhythm.

Glossary

This glossary of political terms (and the subsequent short biographies and outline of the events following the delivery of the *De Imperio*) are included to give a complete view of the context of the speech and to help with understanding. Candidates for the examination are reminded that questions involving knowledge of these parts of this Introduction will not be set. The examination questions will require discussion only of the prescribed sections of the speech itself.

Aedile magistrates (four elected each year) who were responsible for the administration of the city of Rome, including the organisation of most games and festivals.

Assembly a formal gathering of adult male Roman citizens, summoned by a magistrate, in order to elect magistrates or to vote on laws and the declaration of war. Voting in assemblies was by units rather than a one man, one vote system; the composition of these units tended to favour older men, the wealthy and those registered in country districts.

Auctoritas 'standing' or 'influence'; an attribute arising from prior achievement, possessed by eminent public figures, which made their advice compelling even in the absence of formal power.

Consul the most senior of the annually-elected magistrates; two each year; they held *imperium*, though by the late Republic they tended to remain in Rome during their year in office and then proceed to a province as a pro-magistrate.

Contio an open-air meeting, convened by a magistrate, to hear speeches on legislative proposals and reports of senatorial meetings; anyone could attend.

Cursus honorum a fixed order (quaestor–praetor–consul) in which magistracies should be held, which also determined minimum ages for tenure and intervals between offices. The aedileship and/or tribunate, if held, came between the quaestorship and praetorship.

Equestrian a characteristic determined by the census; the equestrians were members of the wealthiest class, who had not entered the Senate. Many

equestrians were involved in fulfilling public contracts, including those
for tax-collection (see *publicani*).

Felicitas the characteristic of being *felix*, 'fortunate', or 'prosperous'; it can
be translated as 'good luck', to be distinguished from *fortuna*, 'chance' or
'luck' (good or bad).

Imperium the right to command, held by praetors, consuls and the
dictator; in military contexts, the right was unlimited (and could thus
extend to summary execution); it was limited in civilian contexts by
citizens' rights of appeal (*provocatio*), including to a trial.

Kings Rome's rulers in its first centuries; ejected, according to Rome's
understanding of its past, by popular uprising in the late sixth century
BC, leaving a lasting fear of tyrannical aspirations among its political elite.

Legatus this term has two distinct meanings in Roman politics: either an
ambassador or (anglicised as 'legate') a senior military officer. Legates
did not hold *imperium* themselves but were authorised to command
armies and undertake other military tasks through the *imperium* of the
magistrate or ex-magistrate to whom they were attached.

Magistrate the executive officers of the Roman *res publica*, elected by the
votes of adult male citizens; only the wealthiest citizens were permitted
to stand. Most magistracies were tenable for a year only, with strict
limits on the possibility of repeated tenure.

Nobilitas the *nobiles*, men descended from holders of the consulship;
they were the inner circle of the Senate and generally conservative in
outlook.

Novus homo 'new man'; in Roman politics, used of someone who did not
have senatorial ancestors. *Novi* were regularly among those elected to
the quaestorship (and thus senatorial membership) but seldom reached
the highest offices.

Patrician a member of one of the families which had had a monopoly of
political power at the beginning of the Roman Republic. By the end
of the Republic, the status brought no formal political advantage (and
some disadvantages) but remained a potent marker of distinction. Sulla,
Caesar and Clodius were all patricians (though Clodius gave up the
status in order to hold the tribunate of the *plebs*).

Plebs the Roman people, excepting the patricians.

Popularis an adjective describing individuals and behaviour supportive of the rights and benefits of the Roman people as a whole, often with the implication of opposition to senatorial power.

Praetor the second-most senior annually elected magistracy; eight per year. Praetors held *imperium*, but after Sulla were occupied with legal duties (as court presidents) in Rome during their year in office; many would then govern a province as a promagistrate.

Proscriptions the process, instituted by Sulla in 82–81, of naming enemies of the state, who thereby lost the protection of the laws (hence could be killed with impunity); their property was confiscated. The triumvirs instituted a second round of proscriptions in 43–42, during which Cicero was killed.

Publicani those involved in managing public contracts.

Scientia 'knowledge' or 'understanding'.

Senate in theory, the magistrates' advisory body, composed of ex-magistrates; in practice, its decrees had the force of law provided they were not vetoed. Decisions about foreign policy tended to be made by the Senate.

Tribunus plebis (*also* tribune) an office elected by the *plebs* with the function of defending the interests of the *plebs*. By the late Republic, this office was considered as a magistracy, part of the *cursus honorum*, and bringing with it membership of the Senate.

Triumph a religious procession, culminating in a sacrifice to Jupiter on the Capitoline, led by a victorious general. It was awarded by the Senate and was one of the most significant individual achievements in the Republic.

Virtus the characteristic of being a *vir*, a man (as opposed to a woman); courage; by extension, virtue more generally.

Descriptive Index of Persons

(All dates BC except where noted.)

This descriptive index of persons is provided for reference and to support understanding of the Introduction: detailed knowledge of these biographies will not be tested in the examination.

M. Aemilius Lepidus (c. 120–77): consul in 78; as proconsul, he led an
　　unsuccessful insurrection against Rome and died soon after. His son
　　was one of the triumvirs, with Marcus Antonius and Octavian.

C. Antonius (before 106–after 42): son of the consul of 99; Cicero's
　　colleague as consul in 63; defeated Catiline's forces early in 62; exiled
　　following conviction on extortion charges, 59; recalled from exile by
　　Caesar; censor in 42.

M. Antonius (143–87): leading orator of his generation; consul in 99 BC;
　　killed by Marius' followers in 87.

M. Antonius Creticus (before 113–71): son of the consul of 99; praetor in
　　74; as promagistrate, given *imperium* against the pirates; defeated in 72
　　or 71 and died soon afterwards.

M. Antonius (83–30) ('Mark Antony'): son of the praetor of 74; consul
　　in 44; triumvir with Octavian and Lepidus from 43; after uneasy
　　cooperation in the early 30s, moved to open conflict with Octavian;
　　defeated at the Battle of Actium, 31, and committed suicide in Egypt the
　　following year.

Q. Caecilius Metellus Creticus (c. 111–after 54): consul in 69; campaigned
　　then against the Cretan pirates and clashed with Pompeius during the
　　latter's pirate campaign; eventually received a triumph and the surname
　　'Creticus'.

Q. Caecilius Metellus Pius (c. 130–64/63): supporter of Sulla; consul 80;
　　pontifex maximus from 81 until death; campaigned in Spain during the
　　70s against Sertorius and triumphed.

P. Clodius (late 90s–52): patrician by birth; adopted by a plebeian in order
　　to stand for the tribunate of the *plebs* (the spelling 'Clodius' instead
　　of 'Claudius' may indicate popular sympathies); vigorous opponent
　　of Cicero, whose exile he secured as tribune in 58; responsible for
　　extensive and significant *popularis* legislation; murdered in 52 whilst
　　campaigning for the praetorship

L. Cornelius Cinna (c. 130–84); patrician; consul in 87; driven out of Rome
　　and deposed from office because of opposition to Sulla's acts; seized
　　Rome by force in cooperation with Marius; held consulship again in
　　86–84, attempting to re-establish peaceful government in Italy; killed by
　　his troops as he prepared for Sulla's return to Italy.

L. Cornelius Sulla (138–78): patrician; consul in 88; appointed initially as commander against Mithridates, but lost the command to Marius through a popular vote; seized Rome by force as consul in 88 and exiled Marius and his allies. Campaign against Mithridates compromised by political dissensions in Rome; returned to Italy in winter of 84/83; defeated his opponents in November 82 at the Battle of the Colline Gate; appointed dictator; proscribed his opponents and carried through a radical programme of political reform.

A. Gabinius (c. 110–47): as tribune of the *plebs* in 67 proposed the law which gave Pompeius command against the pirates; served as legate in Pompeius' campaign against Mithridates; consul in 58, when he earned Cicero's hatred by failing to support him against Clodius; proconsul in Syria; convicted on extortion charges after his return; recalled by Caesar, and fought on his side during the civil war; died of illness in 47.

Q. Hortensius Hortalus (114–50): leading orator in the immediate post-Sullan period; defended Verres; consul 69.

C. Iulius Caesar (100–44): patrician; consul 59; proconsul in Gaul, 58–50, and author of *De Bello Gallico*; invaded Italy in 49 to secure continuing political eminence; defeated Pompeius at the Battle of Pharsalus in 48 and remaining opposition in Africa in 46 and Spain in 45; appointed dictator for life shortly before he was assassinated by a large senatorial conspiracy in March 44.

M. Licinius Crassus (before 112–53): Pompeius' colleague as consul in 70 and 55; obtained Syria as proconsular command after second consulship, attacked the Parthians, and was defeated and killed at the Battle of Carrhae in 53.

L. Licinius Lucullus (before 116–56): consul 74; conducted Third Mithridatic war, 73–67; recalled following failures.

Q. Lutatius Catulus (before 120–61 or 60): consul 78 and censor in 65; leading politician in the post-Sullan period.

C. Manilius (c. 110–after 65): as tribune of the *plebs* in 66 proposed a law giving Pompeius *imperium* against Mithridates and Tigranes; convicted of treason (*maiestas*) in 65 and exiled.

C. Marius (c. 157–86): *novus homo*; reached the consulship in 107 and brought the war against Jugurtha to an end; repeated tenure of the consulship, 104–100, during which period he campaigned against the Gauls in northern Italy and southern France; his great popularity was dented through his opposition to the tribune Saturninus; attempted to secure command against Mithridates in 88 and returned from exile in 87 to seize Rome with Cinna; died early in his seventh consulship in 86.

Mithridates (120s–63): Mithridates VI of Pontus; invaded the province of Asia in 88; intermittently at war with Rome thereafter until his death.

Octavian (63–AD 14): more properly, C. Iulius Caesar Octavianus, but known as Octavian in English to prevent confusion with his great-uncle (and, posthumously, adoptive father) Julius Caesar; triumvir from 43 with Mark Antony and Lepidus; defeated Antony at Actium in 31; took name 'Augustus' in 27; sole ruler from then until death, though attempted to maintain some form of constitutional government.

Cn. Papirius Carbo (before 127–82 or 81): Cinna's colleague as consul in 85 and 84; coordinated opposition to Sulla after Cinna's death; captured and executed by Pompeius in 82 or 81.

Cn. Pompeius Magnus (106–48): son of Cn. Pompeius Strabo (consul 89); joined Sulla's invasion of Italy, 84–82, and was rewarded with *imperium* despite not having held a qualifying office; employed by Sulla to defeat his enemies in Sicily and Africa, 82–81, and then by the Senate to put down Lepidus' revolt (77) and complete the defeat of Sertorius in Spain (77–71); consul in 70, when he supported *popularis* measures; held a special command against the pirates (67) and Mithridates and Tigranes (66–62); collaborated with Caesar during the latter's consulship (59); consul again in 55 and 52; opposed Caesar's demand for a second consulship (49); leader of the anti-Caesarian forces (49–48); defeated at the Battle of Pharsalus (48) and killed later that year while seeking refuge in Egypt.

Cn. Pompeius Strabo (before 131–87): consul in 89; commanded forces during the Social War, captured Asculum Picenum during his consulship and triumphed; attempted to hold a second, consecutive consulship; did not give up his army command and played a prominent role in the civil war of 88–87 before dying of an epidemic disease; very unpopular with the Roman people.

C. Sempronius Gracchus (c. 153–121): younger brother of the tribune of

133; held the tribunate in 123 and 122; sponsored a broad programme
of *popularis* legislation but lost support when he proposed to extend
the Roman citizenship; killed during senatorial repression following
violence after he failed to be re-elected.

Ti. Sempronius Gracchus (c. 163–133): as tribune of the *plebs* in 133 put
forward a law on land tenure which challenged the interests of the
wealthy; killed by a senatorial mob while seeking re-election as tribune;
became exemplary of *popularis* political action.

L. Sergius Catilina (before 105–62) (commonly known in English as
Catiline): supporter of Sulla; failed to be elected consul for 63, and
during 63 began an armed uprising against Rome; killed in battle early
in 62.

M. Terentius Varro (116–27): supporter and legate of Pompeius, for whom
he wrote a manual on senatorial procedure; fought against Caesar
during the civil war and was pardoned; proscribed in 43, though
survived; prolific scholar and writer, of whose extensive works only
De Re Rustica survives entire.

Tigranes (c. 120–c. 56): king of Armenia; son-in-law and ally of
Mithridates VI; pursued expansionist foreign policy in Antolia and
Mesopotamia until defeated by Pompeius (66); recognised by Rome as
king of Armenia and remained a Roman ally until his death.

M. Tullius Cicero (106–43): *novus homo*; leading forensic orator; reached
consulship in 63; instrumental in uncovering and defeating Catiline's
plot, but exiled in 58 because he had executed citizens without trial;
recalled from exile in 57, but failed to re-establish political authority;
sided reluctantly with Pompeius during civil war; pardoned by Caesar,
and turned to philosophy; after Caesar's assassination opposed Mark
Antony's ambitions and was proscribed and killed in 43.

Timeline

132–130	Rome establishes its rule in Asia.
120	Mithridates becomes king of Pontus.
88	Mithridates' invasion of Asia. Sulla leads Roman forces during inconclusive First Mithridatic War, ended by Peace of Dardanus in 85.
83–81	Second Mithridatic War.
82–80	Sulla's dictatorship; proscriptions and constitutional change at Rome.
77	Lepidus' uprising.
71	End of war in Spain.
70	First consulship of Pompeius and Crassus.
67	*Lex Gabinia* appointing Pompeius against the pirates. Lucullus' command ended.
66	*Lex Manilia* appointing Pompeius to campaign against Mithridates and Tigranes.
65	Manilius convicted on *maiestas* charges.
63	Pompeius reached Jerusalem; death of Mithridates VI. Cicero and Antonius consuls; Catiline's uprising.
59	Consulship of Caesar.
58	Clodius' tribunate; Cicero exiled.
55	Second consulship of Pompeius and Crassus.
53	Death of Crassus at Carrhae.
49	Civil war between Caesar and Pompeius begins.
48	Caesar victorious at Pharsalus; Pompeius killed in Egypt.
44	Caesar assassinated. Cicero begins *Philippics*.
43	Formation of triumvirate. Proscriptions. Death of Cicero.

Further Reading

Braund, S. M., 'Praise and Protreptic in Early Imperial Panegyric: Cicero, Seneca, Pliny', in R. Rees, ed., *Oxford Readings in Classical Studies: Latin Panegyric* (Oxford, 2012), 85–108.

Includes a discussion of Cicero's influence on the panegyrists.

Hölkeskamp, K.-J., *Reconstructing the Roman Republic: An Ancient Political Culture and Modern Research* (Princeton, 2010).

Stimulating and polemical essay on the 'democratic turn' in research on the Roman Republic, which also provides an introduction to major contributions by scholars writing in languages other than English.

Jehne, M., 'Feeding the *Plebs* with Words: The Significance of Senatorial Public Oratory in the Small World of Roman Politics', in C. Steel and H. van der Blom, eds, *Community and Communication: Oratory and Politics in Republican Rome* (Oxford, 2013), 49–62.

Discussion of deliberative speech which concentrates on the *De imperio Cn. Pompei*.

MacCormack, S., 'Cicero in Late Antiquity', in C. Steel, ed., *The Cambridge Companion to Cicero* (Cambridge, 2013), 251–305.

Extensive and scholarly treatment of Cicero's readers and influence in late antiquity, which includes observations on the fate of *De imperio*.

Morstein-Marx, R., *Mass Oratory and Political Power in the Late Roman Republic* (Cambridge, 2004).

Incisive analysis of the role of oratory in late Republican politics.

Powell, J., 'Cicero's style', in C. Steel, ed., *The Cambridge Companion to Cicero* (Cambridge, 2013), 41–72.

Analysis of Cicero's stylistic choices across his writings, with many examples.

Rawson, E., 'Caesar's Heritage: Hellenistic Kings and their Roman Equals', *Journal of Roman Studies* 65 (1975): 148–59.

Wide-ranging discussion of regal imagery in Roman politics.

Seager, R., *Pompey the Great*, 2nd edn (London, 2002).

Standard biography in English on Pompeius.

Steel, C., *The End of the Roman Republic, 146–44 B.C.: Conquest and Crisis* (Edinburgh, 2013).

Narrative history of the period.

Tempest, K., *Cicero: Politics and Persuasion in Ancient Rome* (London, 2011).

Good recent biography with a strong emphasis on oratory.

http://rhetoric.byu.edu/

The 'Silva Rhetoricae' site hosted at Brigham Young University; includes a descriptive index of rhetorical figures.

Text

27. Satis mihi multa verba fecisse videor, quare esset hoc bellum genere ipso necessarium, magnitudine periculosum: restat ut de imperatore ad id bellum deligendo ac tantis rebus praeficiendo dicendum esse videatur. utinam, Quirites, virorum fortium atque innocentium copiam tantam haberetis, ut haec vobis deliberatio difficilis esset, quemnam potissimum tantis rebus ac tanto bello praeficiendum putaretis! nunc vero cum sit unus Cn. Pompeius, qui non modo eorum hominum, qui nunc sunt, gloriam, sed etiam antiquitatis memoriam virtute superarit, quae res est quae cuiusquam animum in hac causa dubium facere possit?

28. Ego enim sic existimo, in summo imperatore quattuor has res inesse oportere: scientiam rei militaris, virtutem, auctoritatem, felicitatem. quis igitur hoc homine scientior umquam aut fuit aut esse debuit? qui e ludo atque pueritiae disciplinis, bello maximo atque acerrimis hostibus, ad patris exercitum atque in militiae disciplinam profectus est; qui extrema pueritia miles in exercitu fuit summi imperatoris, ineunte adulescentia maximi ipse exercitus imperator; qui saepius cum hoste conflixit quam quisquam cum inimico concertavit, plura bella gessit quam ceteri legerunt, plures provincias confecit quam alii concupiverunt; cuius adulescentia ad scientiam rei militaris non alienis praeceptis sed suis imperiis, non offensionibus belli sed victoriis, non stipendiis sed triumphis est erudita. quod denique genus esse belli potest, in quo illum non exercuerit fortuna rei publicae? civile, Africanum, Transalpinum, Hispaniense, servile, navale bellum, varia et diversa genera et bellorum et hostium, non solum gesta ab hoc uno, sed etiam confecta nullam rem esse declarant in usu positam militari, quae huius viri scientiam fugere possit.

29. Iam vero virtuti Cn. Pompei quae potest oratio par inveniri? quid est quod quisquam aut illo dignum aut vobis novum aut cuiquam inauditum possit adferre? neque enim illae sunt solae virtutes imperatoriae, quae vulgo existimantur, labor in negotiis, fortitudo in periculis, industria in agendo, celeritas in conficiendo, consilium in providendo, quae tanta sunt in hoc uno, quanta in omnibus reliquis imperatoribus, quos aut vidimus aut audivimus, non fuerunt.

30. Testis est Italia, quam ille ipse victor L. Sulla huius virtute et subsidio confessus est liberatam: testis est Sicilia, quam multis undique cinctam periculis non terrore belli, sed consilii celeritate explicavit: testis est Africa, quae magnis oppressa hostium copiis eorum ipsorum sanguine redundavit: testis est Gallia, per quam legionibus nostris iter in Hispaniam Gallorum internicione patefactum est: testis est Hispania, quae saepissime plurimos hostes ab hoc superatos prostratosque conspexit: testis est iterum et saepius Italia, quae cum servili bello taetro periculosoque premeretur, ab hoc auxilium absente expetivit, quod bellum exspectatione eius attenuatum atque imminutum est, adventu sublatum ac sepultum.

31. Testes nunc vero iam omnes orae atque omnes exterae gentes ac nationes, denique maria omnia, cum universa, tum in singulis oris omnes sinus atque portus. quis enim toto mari locus per hos annos aut tam firmum habuit praesidium, ut tutus esset, aut tam fuit abditus, ut lateret? quis navigavit, qui non se aut mortis aut servitutis periculo committeret, cum aut hieme aut referto praedonum mari navigaret? hoc tantum bellum, tam turpe, tam vetus, tam late divisum atque dispersum quis umquam arbitraretur aut ab omnibus imperatoribus uno anno aut omnibus annis ab uno imperatore confici posse?

32. Quam provinciam tenuistis a praedonibus liberam per hosce annos? quod vectigal vobis tutum fuit? quem socium defendistis? cui praesidio classibus vestris fuistis? quam multas existimatis insulas

esse desertas, quam multas aut metu relictas aut a praedonibus captas urbes esse sociorum? sed quid ego longinqua commemoro? fuit hoc quondam, fuit proprium populi Romani, longe a domo bellare et propugnaculis imperii sociorum fortunas, non sua tecta defendere. sociis ego nostris mare per hosce annos clausum fuisse dicam, cum exercitus vestri numquam Brundisio nisi hieme summa transmiserint? qui ad vos ab exteris nationibus venirent, captos querar, cum legati populi Romani redempti sint? mercatoribus tutum mare non fuisse dicam, cum duodecim secures in praedonum potestatem pervenerint?

33. Cnidum aut Colophonem aut Samum, nobilissimas urbes, innumerabilesque alias captas esse commemorem, cum vestros portus atque eos portus, quibus vitam et spiritum ducitis, in praedonum fuisse potestate sciatis? an vero ignoratis portum Caietae celeberrimum ac plenissimum navium inspectante praetore a praedonibus esse direptum? ex Miseno autem eius ipsius liberos, qui cum praedonibus antea bellum gesserat, a praedonibus esse sublatos? nam quid ego Ostiense incommodum atque illam labem atque ignominiam rei publicae querar, cum prope inspectantibus vobis classis ea, cui consul populi Romani praepositus esset, a praedonibus capta atque oppressa est? Pro di immortales! tantamne unius hominis incredibilis ac divina virtus tam brevi tempore lucem adferre rei publicae potuit, ut vos, qui modo ante ostium Tiberinum classem hostium videbatis, nunc nullam intra Oceani ostium praedonum navem esse audiatis?

34. Atque haec qua celeritate gesta sint, quamquam videtis, tamen a me in dicendo praetereunda non sunt. quis enim umquam aut obeundi negotii aut consequendi quaestus studio tam brevi tempore tot loca adire, tantos cursus conficere potuit, quam celeriter Cn. Pompeio duce tanti belli impetus navigavit? qui nondum tempestivo ad navigandum mari Siciliam adiit, Africam exploravit, in Sardiniam cum classe venit, atque haec tria frumentaria subsidia rei publicae firmissimis praesidiis classibusque munivit.

35. Inde cum se in Italiam recepisset, duabus Hispaniis et Gallia Transalpina praesidiis ac navibus confirmata, missis item in oram Illyrici maris et in Achaiam omnemque Graeciam navibus Italiae duo maria maximis classibus firmissimisque praesidiis adornavit, ipse autem, ut Brundisio profectus est, undequinquagesimo die totam ad imperium populi Romani Ciliciam adiunxit: omnes, qui ubique praedones fuerunt, partim capti interfectique sunt, partim unius huius se imperio ac potestati dediderunt. idem Cretensibus, cum ad eum usque in Pamphyliam legatos deprecatoresque misissent, spem deditionis non ademit obsidesque imperavit. ita tantum bellum, tam diuturnum, tam longe lateque dispersum, quo bello omnes gentes ac nationes premebantur, Cn. Pompeius extrema hieme apparavit, ineunte vere suscepit, media aestate confecit.

36. Est haec divina atque incredibilis virtus imperatoris: quid? ceterae, quas paulo ante commemorare coeperam, quantae atque quam multae sunt! non enim bellandi virtus solum in summo ac perfecto imperatore quaerenda est, sed multae sunt artes eximiae huius administrae comitesque virtutis. ac primum quanta innocentia debent esse imperatores! quanta deinde in omnibus rebus temperantia! quanta fide, quanta facilitate, quanto ingenio, quanta humanitate! quae breviter qualia sint in Cn. Pompeio consideremus; summa enim omnia sunt, Quirites, sed ea magis ex aliorum contentione quam ipsa per sese cognosci atque intellegi possunt.

37. Quem enim imperatorem possumus ullo in numero putare, cuius in exercitu centuriatus veneant atque venierint? quid hunc hominem magnum aut amplum de re publica cogitare, qui pecuniam ex aerario depromptam ad bellum administrandum aut propter cupiditatem provinciae magistratibus diviserit aut propter avaritiam Romae in quaestu reliquerit? vestra admurmuratio facit, Quirites, ut agnoscere videamini, qui haec fecerint: ego autem nomino neminem; quare irasci mihi nemo poterit, nisi qui ante de se voluerit confiteri.

itaque propter hanc avaritiam imperatorum quantas calamitates, quocumque ventum est, nostri exercitus ferant, quis ignorat?

38. Itinera, quae per hosce annos in Italia per agros atque oppida civium Romanorum nostri imperatores fecerint, recordamini: tum facilius statuetis, quid apud exteras nationes fieri existimetis. utrum plures arbitramini per hosce annos militum vestrorum armis hostium urbes an hibernis sociorum civitates esse deletas? neque enim potest exercitum is continere imperator, qui se ipse non continet, neque severus esse in iudicando, qui alios in se severos esse iudices non vult.

39. Hic miramur hunc hominem tantum excellere ceteris, cuius legiones sic in Asiam pervenerint, ut non modo manus tanti exercitus, sed ne vestigium quidem cuiquam pacato nocuisse dicatur? iam vero quem ad modum milites hibernent, cotidie sermones ac litterae perferuntur. non modo ut sumptum faciat in militem nemini vis adfertur, sed ne cupienti quidem cuiquam permittitur. hiemis enim, non avaritiae perfugium maiores nostri in sociorum atque amicorum tectis esse voluerunt.

40. Age vero ceteris in rebus qua ille sit temperantia, considerate. unde illam tantam celeritatem et tam incredibilem cursum inventum putatis? non enim illum eximia vis remigum aut ars inaudita quaedam gubernandi aut venti aliqui novi tam celeriter in ultimas terras pertulerunt, sed eae res, quae ceteros remorari solent, non retardarunt: non avaritia ab instituto cursu ad praedam aliquam devocavit, non libido ad voluptatem, non amoenitas ad delectationem, non nobilitas urbis ad cognitionem, non denique labor ipse ad quietem; postremo signa et tabulas ceteraque ornamenta Graecorum oppidorum, quae ceteri tollenda esse arbitrantur, ea sibi ille ne visenda quidem existimavit.

41. Itaque omnes nunc in iis locis Cn. Pompeium sicut aliquem non ex hac urbe missum, sed de caelo delapsum intuentur; nunc denique incipiunt credere, fuisse homines Romanos hac quondam continentia,

quod iam nationibus exteris incredibile ac falso memoriae proditum videbatur; nunc imperii vestri splendor illis gentibus lucem adferre coepit; nunc intellegunt non sine causa maiores suos tum, cum ea temperantia magistratus habebamus, servire populo Romano quam imperare aliis maluisse. iam vero ita faciles aditus ad eum privatorum, ita liberae querimoniae de aliorum iniuriis esse dicuntur, ut is qui dignitate principibus excellit, facilitate infimis par esse videatur.

42. Iam quantum consilio, quantum dicendi gravitate et copia valeat, in quo ipso inest quaedam dignitas imperatoria, vos, Quirites, hoc ipso ex loco saepe cognovistis. fidem vero eius quantam inter socios existimari putatis, quam hostes omnes omnium generum sanctissimam iudicarint? humanitate iam tanta est, ut difficile dictu sit, utrum hostes magis virtutem eius pugnantes timuerint an mansuetudinem victi dilexerint. et quisquam dubitabit quin huic hoc tantum bellum permittendum sit, qui ad omnia nostrae memoriae bella conficienda divino quodam consilio natus esse videatur?

43. Et quoniam auctoritas quoque in bellis administrandis multum atque in imperio militari valet, certe nemini dubium est quin ea re idem ille imperator plurimum possit. vehementer autem pertinere ad bella administranda, quid hostes, quid socii de imperatoribus nostris existiment, quis ignorat, cum sciamus homines in tantis rebus, ut aut contemnant aut metuant, aut oderint aut ament, opinione non minus et fama quam aliqua ratione certa commoveri? quod igitur nomen umquam in orbe terrarum clarius fuit? cuius res gestae pares? de quo homine vos, id quod maxime facit auctoritatem, tanta et tam praeclara iudicia fecistis?

44. An vero ullam usquam esse oram tam desertam putatis, quo non illius diei fama pervaserit, cum universus populus Romanus referto foro completisque omnibus templis, ex quibus hic locus conspici potest, unum sibi ad commune omnium gentium bellum

Cn. Pompeium imperatorem depoposcit? itaque, ut plura non dicam neque aliorum exemplis confirmem, quantum auctoritas valeat in bello, ab eodem Cn Pompeio omnium rerum egregiarum exempla sumantur: qui quo die a vobis maritimo bello praepositus est imperator, tanta repente vilitas annonae ex summa inopia et caritate rei frumentariae consecuta est unius hominis spe ac nomine, quantum vix in summa ubertate agrorum diuturna pax efficere potuisset.

45. Iam accepta in Ponto calamitate ex eo proelio, de quo vos paulo ante invitus admonui, cum socii pertimuissent, hostium opes animique crevissent, satis firmum praesidium provincia non haberet, amisissetis Asiam, Quirites, nisi ad ipsum discrimen eius temporis divinitus Cn. Pompeium ad eas regiones fortuna populi Romani attulisset. huius adventus et Mithridatem insolita inflatum victoria continuit et Tigranem magnis copiis minitantem Asiae retardavit. et quisquam dubitabit, quid virtute perfecturus sit, qui tantum auctoritate perfecerit? aut quam facile imperio atque exercitu socios et vectigalia conservaturus sit, qui ipso nomine ac rumore defenderit?

Notes

Chapter 27

mihi ... videor – 'I seem to myself' and so 'I think that I ...' Cicero adopts here an unassuming and humble tone.

quare – 'as to why...' *quare* introduces an indirect question, hence the subjunctive *esset*.

necessarium ... periculosum ... – Cicero refers here to the first two stages of his *argumentatio* in which he discussed the nature of the war and its size, and concluded that it was therefore both necessary and dangerous (see Introduction, p. 20). The discussion of the choice of commander is the third and final stage of the *argumentatio*.

de imperatore ... deligendo ... praeficiendo – by the process known as gerundive attraction, Cicero uses here a noun described by a gerundive, rather than a gerund with a direct object. English, however, prefers to avoid the passive and to keep the sense active instead: 'about the choice ... and appointment ... of a commander'.

ut ... dicendum esse videatur – notice the meaning of *ut* + subjunctive here – 'that...' *dicendum* is a gerundive of obligation, used impersonally (and so in the third sg neuter form) – '... it seems necessary to discuss'. *videatur* continues with the humble tone established at the start of the chapter.

Quirites – this title has its origin in the inhabitants of the Sabine town Cures, but after the union of the Romans and the Sabines, it became the standard way to address Roman citizens in their civil capacity (for more on the citizens' role within the structure of the Roman state, see Introduction, 'The Roman *Res Publica*').

fortium ... innocentium – Cicero sets out the two key strands of his argument for Pompeius' suitability: that he is exceptionally able as a military commander, and that his blameless nature will ensure that he acts in the public interest (see Introduction for the possible threat posed to the state by individuals with exceptional military powers).

quemnam ... putaretis – the indirect question explains *haec deliberatio* – 'the decision as to whom ...'. *–nam* as a suffix at the start of a question was used to add emphasis.

praeficiendum – gerundive of obligation (*esse* has been left out).

cum sit – the verb 'to be' used at the start of a sentence or clause denotes existence – 'since there is ...'; **unus** – emphatic, and in contrast to *copiam tantam*.

nunc vero – 'but as things are'.

virtute superarit – *superarit* is the shortened form of the perfect subjunctive *superaverit*, and used after *qui* to create a sort of result clause denoting that this is the consequence of Pompeius' nature / character (known as a 'generic *qui*-clause'): Pompeius is such a man that he has ... *virtute* – instrumental ablative – 'by means of his ...'

virtus is presented here as the cornerstone of Cicero's argument in favour of appointing Pompeius to this extraordinary command: *virtus* is wide-reaching in its meaning, but in essence refers to the values and skills needed to excel as a man, and indeed therefore as a successful military commander (see Glossary). In the course of this speech, Cicero makes use of the full scope of the meaning of *virtus*, moving from manly / military excellence to a wider sense of moral virtue (see Chapter 36).

quae ... possit – again, the relative pronoun + subjunctive to create a generic *qui*-clause (see above) – 'such as could ...'.

Chapter 28

ego ... existimo – *ego* for emphasis: Cicero's tone has become more assertive.

scientiam rei militaris, virtutem, auctoritatem, felicitatem – Cicero gives these as the four qualities that should belong to a military commander, and uses them as a structure for the praise for Pompeius which follows (see Introduction, p. 22). All are accusative since they are set in apposition to *quattuor has res*.

As mentioned above, Pompeius' *virtus* takes centre stage in Cicero's argument, and this can be seen from the different amounts of time and attention he gives to these four qualities in turn. His discussion of *scientia rei militaris* runs until the end of this chapter; the discussion of *virtus* as military excellence begins in Chapter 29, keeps going for seven chapters and then from Chapter 36 is developed into a discussion of the accompanying *artes virtutis*; the discussion of *auctoritas* begins in Chapter 43, and the concluding discussion of *felicitas* occupies only chapters 47 and 48.

scientior – marks the first of the four sections in praise of Pompeius. *scientia* refers to the sort of technical knowledge which comes from experience, understanding and skill; the argument here is that Pompeius' exceptional military experience to date means that his *scientia* surpasses all others'.

fuit – notice the choice of tense: the perfect of *esse* is used for completed past states – Cicero here is picking up on his reference to *antiquitatis memoriam* and referring to previous (and now no-longer alive) commanders.

esse debuit – 'ought to have been'.

qui – *qui, quae, quod* can be used at the start of a sentence to pick up upon a noun in the previous sentence that was not the subject; used thus it is known as the 'connecting relative' and it is best translated as 'he / she / it' or 'this'. Here it refers back to *hoc homine* (Pompeius), and is repeated a further three times (*qui ... qui ... cuius ...*).

bello maximo atque acerrimis hostibus – ablatives of attendant circumstances – 'in a very great war, and against the fiercest enemies' – and probably a reference to Pompeius' father's military command in the Social War of 91–89 BC, when Pompeius was one of his military staff (see Introduction, p. 9). The Social War was bitterly destructive (Velleius Paterculus gives the death toll as in excess of 300,000 – see 2.15.3), and it is perfectly possible that some of those listening to this speech were the children of those enfranchised as Roman citizens at its end, or enfranchised themselves. It is no surprise, therefore, that the reference here is vague.

summi imperatoris – probably a reference to Strabo (see Descriptive Index of Persons).

maximi ipse exercitus imperator – probably a reference to 84–83 BC and the civil war in which Sulla appointed Pompeius as commander of one of his armies (see Introduction, p. 10). It is worth noting that in these references, Cicero seems to have elided the gap between the end of the Social War (in 88) and Pompeius' association with Sulla in 84/83: for the period in between, Pompeius had associated with Cinna (see Descriptive Index of Persons) and Carbo. Cinna was murdered by his troops in 84 BC, and by the time of this speech his posthumous reputation was distinctly unpopular; Cicero seems here to be avoiding anything which pulls too obviously against his glowing presentation of Pompeius' character and actions.

cum hoste conflixit ... cum inimico concertavit – a neat contrast between military combat and private lawsuits: the latter were the more usual means by which aspiring Roman nobles achieved fame and status through a demonstration of their oratorical skills (see Introduction on *Language and Style*), and so built up their political career to the point where they might be granted military commands; Pompeius on the other hand – through his remarkable and early military appointments / experience – has used this as the elementary stages of his military / political career.

plura bella gessit quam ceteri legerunt – a similar contrast: Pompeius' education has been in fighting wars, others' education has been through reading of them.

plures provincias confecit quam alii concupiverunt – *provincia* here in the sense of 'task', and so *confecit* as 'discharged'. It is during this century that the word *provincia* seems to have shifted in its meaning from 'task' or 'job' to 'province', and it is likely that this change was the result of the shift in Rome's imperialism from a system of giving orders to local communities and rulers to one of more direct territorial control and Roman provincial rulers (see Introduction, p. 6).

stipendiis ... triumphis – *stipendium* originally referred to military pay, and so came to mean a period of military service; a *triumphus* was the celebratory procession through Rome granted by the senate to a general after a significant victory (see Glossary). Cicero is drawing attention to the fact that Pompeius had held two triumphs: very few men did that, and none so young as Pompeius.

fortuna rei publicae – 'the fortunes of our state' – notice that Cicero is laying the foundations for his *popularis* approach: Pompeius' life to date has already been tied up with the successes of the Roman state, and the benefits therefore for the Roman people.

civile, Africanum, Transalpinum, Hispaniense, servile, navale bellum – a pounding list to conclude Cicero's description of Pompeius' previous military experience (see Introduction, pp. 9–13 for more details). All are nominative, are summarised by *varia et diversa genera*, then further described by the participles *gesta ... confecta* and – personified – they act as the subjects for *declarant*.

Chapter 29

Here begins the second and the longest of the four sections in praise of Pompeius. As introduced in Chapter 27, Cicero moves from his description of Pompeius' *scientia* to a description of his *virtus*. To begin with, Cicero focuses on Pompeius' military brilliance and offers a rapid sweep of his previous military success in Italy, Sicily, Africa, Gaul, Spain and – in an extended rhetorical climax – against the pirates (see Introduction, pp. 11–13 for more details).

iam vero – *iam* marks the beginning of a new section, and *vero* emphasises this.

quae – interrogative adjective in agreement with *oratio* – 'what speech ...'.

cuiquam – dative of person affected (just as *vobis*), but in effect the agent for *inauditum* and so 'unheard of by anyone'.

neque ... illae sunt solae virtutes imperatoriae – *illae* refers forward to the list *labor ... fortitudo ... industria ... celeritas ... consilium* and so 'the virtues of a general are not only those which ...'; **quae** – neuter plural (and so too *tanta ... quanta ...* below) because it refers to all the virtues listed.

negotiis – from *nec/otium* and so refers in general to any sort of work, task or occupation.

tanta ... quanta ... – usually 'as great ... as ...' but followed here by the negative *non fuerunt* and so better translated as 'greater [in this one man] than they have been ...'.

Chapter 30

Testis est Italia – Cicero refers here to 84–83 BC when Sulla returned to Italy to wage civil war against his enemies: notice that Cicero bypasses the awkward issue of civil war and gives instead a positive spin on war's aftermath (*victor ... liberatam*). For more details on the civil war (and Pompeius' campaigns against Sulla's opponents in Sicily and Africa), see Introduction, p. 10.

quam ... L. Sulla ... confessus est liberatam ... – understand *esse* with *liberatam* to complete the indirect statement after *confessus est*.

ille ipse victor L. Sulla – it is hard to match the emphasis in English – 'the great victor himself Lucius Sulla'.

explicavit – the subject is left out but is, of course, Pompeius.

in Hispaniam – Pompeius was sent to Spain to help defeat Sertorius (see Introduction, p. 10).

legionibus nostris – dative (of advantage after *patefactum est*).

iterum et saepius – 'again and again' – the phrase intensifies the weight already given to *testis est* by the anaphora throughout this section.

cum ... premeretur – a temporal clause within the relative clause (*quae ... expetivit*).

servili bello – the slave war referred to here was the revolt led by Spartacus (see Introduction, p. 10).

absente – agreeing with *hoc* – 'in his absence'.

quod bellum – *bellum* has been attracted into the relative clause, but it picks up on *servili bello* above and should be translated before *quod* 'a war which ...'.

sublatum ac sepultum – understand *est*. There seems little justification for Cicero's claim here; the war was largely over by the time Pompeius arrived.

Chapter 31

nunc vero iam – a stronger form of **iam vero** (see note on Chapter 29), and it heralds the start of the extended section in praise of Pompeius' victory against the pirates (see Introduction, pp. 11–13). Cicero focuses on the extent, severity and the shame of the threat posed by the pirates to Rome and her empire, and then the phenomenal speed with which Pompeius was victorious.

cum ... tum ... – 'both ... and ...'.

in singulis oris – 'along the individual coastlines'.

quis – interrogative and in agreement with *locus*.

toto mari – local ablative to show place.

habuit – perfect rather than the more usual imperfect to show something which was true, but is so no longer.

quis – this time the interrogative pronoun and so 'who…?'.

qui … committeret – *qui* + subjunctive for another generic *qui* clause (see note on *superarit*, Chapter 27). Notice that *qui non* is used here instead of *quin*, which is more often used to introduce this sort of negative consecutive clause.

cum … navigaret – *cum* is causal here, so 'since …'; **aut … aut …** – used for mutually exclusive alternatives, i.e., the point is that the only options were to sail in winter, or when the sea was full of pirates. *hieme* – ablative of time within which; *referto … mari* – ablative absolute.

quis umquam arbitraretur – 'who ever would have thought'.

Chapter 32

tenuistis – Cicero increases the intensity of his rhetoric by a shift in this chapter to a series of direct questions addressed to the Roman people.

per hosce annos – *hosce* is a strengthed form of *hos* (vestiges of the deictic particle –*ce* can be seen in other forms, such as *huic*).

cui praesidio classibus vestris fuistis – *cui* is dative of the interrogative pronoun, and *praesidio* is a predicative dative (commonly used for abstract nouns following the verb 'to be' – cf. the common phrase *odio esse*); *classibus vestris* – ablative, and so 'for whom were you a source of protection with your fleets?'.

quid – 'why?'.

longinqua – probably best translated as 'far away' or 'distant'; Cicero is increasing his momentum by signalling that he is about to pick up the pace and the intensity and move on to material that is closer to home for his audience.

fuit – as for *habuit* in Chapter 31, the perfect tense is used here for something that was once true but now is not, and its climactic repetition needs to be captured in English: 'this was once the case, once the characteristic of the Roman people (namely) to ….' **hoc** refers forward to the infinitive *bellare* (hence its neuter gender).

propugnaculis – 'bulwarks' – physical means of protection, i.e., fleets and armies.

sua tecta – *populi Romani* is not the subject of the sentence, but it is the focus, and the use of the reflexive *sua* ('their own') highlights this.

sociis … nostris – dative (of disadvantage).

mare … clausum fuisse dicam – *dicam* is a deliberative subjunctive (i.e., it is used to introduce a question which is presented as having no answer) – 'am I to say …'. There starts here a sequence of four sentences, each with a deliberative question for the main clause, justified by the contents of the *cum* clauses which follow: the idea behind each is that there is no need to go into the sufferings of others, when the very Romans themselves – previously used to war as a. far-flung thing – have suffered even greater indignities at the hands of the pirates. *clausum fuisse* – a perfect passive infinitive, but *fuisse* makes clear (as with *fuit* above) that this is something which was the case, but is not so now.

Brundisio – as is usual for the names of towns and small islands, the ablative case is used without a preposition to show motion away from. Brundisium was one of Rome's most important ports, and offered the shortest crossing to Greece.

nisi hieme summa – ablative of time – 'except in the deepest winter'.

The point is that even the mighty Roman armies only left Brundisium when the weather conditions were bad enough to deter the pirates (although it is worth noting that the historian Cassius Dio writes that not even the winter months were safe from attacks by pirates).

transmiserint – subjunctive after *cum*, and perfect tense because the sentence is primary sequence (i.e. the main verb is not a past tense, and so it cannot be followed by an imperfect or pluperfect subjunctive).

qui … venirent, captos querar – *qui* is missing its antecedent *eos*, which is needed as the subject of *captos* (with *esse* understood); *venirent* is subjunctive in accordance with the rule that all subordinate clauses in indirect speech should have their verbs in the subjunctive; *querar* – another deliberative subjunctive: 'Am I to lament that the men who came … were captured'.

duodecim secures – the axes were carried by lictors, attendants to Rome's most important magistrates, and were symbols of their power. Praetors were entitled to six lictors each in the provinces, and so (by metonymy) the twelve axes here represent two praetors who were captured by pirates. Plutarch gives their names as Sextilius and Bellinus, but nothing more is known about them.

Chapter 33

vestros portus atque eos portus – refers to one and the same set of harbours, further described by the relative clause which follows.

quibus vitam et spiritum ducitis – *ducitis* is indicative, because the relative clause here is explanatory, and so not part of the indirect speech. *vitam* and *spiritum* – a metaphorical reference to the corn supply shipped in from the provinces, and on which Rome depended.

in praedonum ... potestate – *potestate* is the ablative following *in*, but the genitive *praedonum* which follows it has been promoted for emphasis.

an – gives a sceptical tone to the question which follows it.

Caietae – a port on the west coast of Italy. The attack referred to here may be when the praetor M. Antonius Creticus was in command of the fleet based at Misenum and with a brief to deal with the pirates.

Miseno – Misenum was a port on the south-west coast of Italy, and Rome's largest naval base. Plutarch reports that a daughter of M. Antonius (the father of the praetor mentioned above) was captured by pirates on the coast of Italy. **liberos ... sublatos** – understand *esse*, since the construction is another indirect statement following on from *ignoratis* in the previous sentence; the form is plural for singular. **eius ipsius** – antecedent for *qui*, which is followed by the indicative *gesserat* in an explanatory relative clause – see on *ducitis* above.

nam – hard to translate, and probably best omitted – the word marks the return to the repeated structure of a deliberative subjunctive followed by a *cum* clause.

Ostiense – Ostia was at mouth of the Tiber and only 16 miles from Rome. Dio Cassius confirms that it was raided by pirates.

prope inspectantibus vobis – 'while you were all but watching'.

cui consul ... praepositus esset – *cui* refers back to *classis,* and the subjunctive shows that this is a result clause – a fleet 'such that a consul had been put in charge of it' (*classis ea = classis talis*). The point is that the fleet was big enough to warrant a consular command.

capta atque oppressa est – indicative, as is usual when *cum* means 'when' without any sense of 'since', but set in contrast to the previous subjunctives, the change in mood creates a strong end to this section.

Pro di immortales! – 'gods above!'.

tantamne ... potuit – -*ne* marks the (rhetorical) question; *tantam* and *lucem* agree.

modo – 'just recently'.

ut ... audiatis – result clause.

Chapter 34

Atque ... videtis – the word order prioritises *haec* as the point of connection between this section and the last, but to translate the sentence take the order as *atque quamquam videtis qua celeritate haec gesta sint.* **qua** – the interrogative adjective to introduce an indirect question. Cicero is moving from the description of the magnitude of Pompeius' success, to the speed with which he accomplished it.

in dicendo – gerund – 'in speaking' and so 'in [this] speech'.

praetereunda non sunt – gerundive (of obligation) and in agreement with *haec*.

obeundi negotii aut consequendi quaestus studio – *obeundi negotii* – gerundive plus noun both in the genitive case after the noun *studio*, and so too the parallel phrase *consequendi quaestus.* The whole phrase translates as 'in their enthusiasm for conducting business or for obtaining profit'.

quam celeriter – 'as quickly as'.

Cn. Pompeio duce – 'under the leadership of Cn. Pompeius'.

tanti belli impetus navigavit – 'the force of so great a war sailed forth' – Cicero makes *impetus* the subject, and so the focus rests on the power of Pompeius and his fleet.

qui – a connecting relative (i.e., the relative pronoun used at the start of a sentence), and so best translated here as 'he …'.

nondum tempestivo … mari – the ablative of attendant circumstances here denotes time – 'when the sea was not yet seasonable …'.

haec tria frumentaria subsidia rei publicae – 'these three sources of grain for our state'. *subsidium* carries the sense of 'help' or 'support', and so makes clear that Rome depended on corn exports from countries such as these.

Chapter 35

duabus Hispaniis et Gallia Transalpina … confirmata – notice the feminine ablative plural form for *duo*. *confirmata* applies to both *duabus Hispaniis* and *Gallia Transalpina*, but by a process of attraction, agrees with the nearer of the two. The two Spains were *Citerior* and *Ulterior* – 'Nearer' and 'Further'. See map.

missis … navibus – another ablative absolute

Italiae duo maria – the two seas of Italy – the *Mare Superum* on the east coast and the *Mare Inferum* on the west coast.

ut … profectus est – *ut* + indicative to mean 'when …'.

Brundisio – the ablative case denotes 'from'; the preposition is left out, as is usual for names of towns or small islands.

omnes, qui ubique praedones fuerunt – very hyperbolic language – 'all the pirates in the world'.

idem – 'similarly'.

ad eum usque in Pamphyliam – *usque* is emphatic, and implies a great distance ('all the way'); in fact Pamphylia was not particularly far from Crete.

Cretensibus – dative of disadvantage ('he did not take away from the Cretans ...'). The Romans had attacked the Cretan cities on the grounds that they gave shelter to pirates and in 68 they had appointed Q. Caecilius Metellus (subsequently Creticus – see Descriptive Index of Persons) as the commander there; the citizens there, however, decided that Pompeius gave better treatment to those surrendering than Creticus did, and they made an attempt to surrender to him. The fallout from this was only defused when Pompeius was sent off to deal with Mithridates.

obsidesque imperavit – *obsides* is accusative since it refers to the thing ordered, not the people to whom the order is given – 'he demanded hostages'.

Chapter 36

est haec ... multae sunt – this sentence marks the transition from the first part of Cicero's praise of Pompeius' *virtus*: in Chapters 29–35 Cicero takes *virtus* in its sense of military excellence (hence the phrase here *virtus imperatoris*); now he shifts the meaning to include moral virtues. *haec* is retrospective – 'this [then] is his god-like and inconceivable military skill'.

quid? – engages the listener's attention and marks a transition – 'well then'.

ceterae – understand *virtutes*.

quantae atque quam multae sunt – 'how big and how many they are!'.

artes – these are defined in the next three sentences as *innocentia* (integrity), *temperantia* (restraint), *fides* (loyalty), *facilitas* (accessibility), *ingenium* (natural talent), *humanitas* (kindness).

eximiae huius ... virtutis – take all three together 'of this outstanding skill'.

quanta innocentia – descriptive ablative (so too *temperantia*, *fide*, *facilitate*, *ingenio*, *humanitate*), and so *debent esse* + ablative equates to 'must have ...'.

quae – connecting relative – 'these'.

consideremus – an exhortation – 'let us consider'.

Chapter 37

Here begins Cicero's illustration of Pompeius' *innocentia*, shown by the absence of avarice.

Quem ... imperatorem – interrogative – 'which commander'.

ullo in numero putare – literally – 'to consider in any number' and so 'to consider a commander at all'.

centuriatus – nominative plural – 'the posts of centurion'.

veneant ... venierint – present and perfect subjunctive from *veneo* – 'I am on sale'. The verbs are subjunctive because the relative clause is a generic *qui* clause which offers a definition of the sort of man referred to. Corrupt commanders were capable of offering military office to the highest bidder rather than to the most deserving candidate.

quid hunc hominem magnum aut amplum de re publica cogitare, qui ... – understand *possumus putare* from the previous sentence, and then take *hunc hominem* as the accusative subject of *cogitare* and *quid ... magnum aut amplum* as its object; *hunc* looks forward to the definition in the relative clause: 'what great or honourable thought about our state are we able to believe this [sort of] man to have who ...'.

propter cupiditatem provinciae – *provincia* here in its sense of 'office, command'; the reference here is vague, but Cicero is probably referring to attempts to bribe magistrates to stop the appointment of a successor, and so extend the term of office.

Romae – locative – 'at Rome'.

in quaestu – 'in profit' and so 'on loan' (i.e., making profit from the interest paid by others).

facit ... ut ... videamini – literally 'makes it that you seem' and so 'shows that you ...'.

qui haec fecerint – an indirect question (after *agnoscere*).

nisi qui ante ... voluerit – 'who does not wish first ...'; *ante* is in place of *antea*. *voluerit* is a future perfect indicative, but best translated as a present tense, as is usual in English for many subordinate clauses which refer to the future.

quantas calamitates ... nostri exercitus ferant – '[who is unaware of] what great disasters our armies bring' – i.e. the damage inflicted on others by the Roman armies led by dishonourable men.

quocumque ventum est – impersonal passive, but – since in this context English has no equivalent idiom – best translated as 'wherever they go' (the verb is indicative because technically the clause is not part of the indirect question).

Chapter 38

Itinera, quae … fecerint – subjunctive for a generic *qui* clause – 'the sort of journeys which …'.

per hosce annos – *hosce* – emphatic form of *hos* (see note on the same phrase in Chapter 32).

civium Romanorum – after the Social War (see Introduction, p. 9) the Italian communities had received Roman citizenship.

recordamini – imperative.

plures – with *hostium urbes* and then (after *an*) *sociorum civitates*.

militum vestrorum – this genitive applies both to *armis* and to *hibernis*: the contrast is between the Roman soldiers out on campaign and at rest in their winter quarters; the latter placed a heavy burden on allied communities, who were expected to fund the cost of these.

neque … non continet – the account of *innocentia* shifts to a discussion of *temperantia*, which is then more formally introduced at the start of Chapter 40.

severus esse – supply *potest* from the first half of the sentence.

Chapter 39

hic – 'in these circumstances'.

tantum – 'to such an extent'.

cuius … pervenerint – a causal relative clause, hence the subjunctive – 'given that his …'.

ut non … sed ne … quidem … dicatur – is the result clause which follows the previous *sic*. *manus* and *vestigium* are both the subjects of *dicatur*, but the verb is singular by attraction to its nearer subject *vestigium*. *manus* – 'armed band' – refers to acts of aggression; *vestigium* in contrast refers to the 'footprint' usually left by an army as it passed through allied communities, i.e. the cost (see above) even without any direct attacks. *non … sed ne … quidem* – 'neither … nor even …'.

cuiquam pacato – 'anyone who had surrendered'.

quem ad modum – 'as to how' – the indirect clause follows *sermones ac litterae* – 'gossip and written reports'.

perferuntur – 'reach us'.

non modo … adfertur … permittitur – notice that although Cicero could easily have written this as reported speech conveying the message of the gossip and written reports, he chooses instead to give it greater weight by presenting it as direct speech.

non modo … adfertur: translate as *non modo vis nemini adfertur ut sumptum in militem faciat.*

sed ne cupienti quidem cuiquam permittitur – 'but not even a man who wants to is allowed [to do so]'. This use of *permitto* is intransitive, and so for the passive, the impersonal construction has to be used.

perfugium – with both *hiemis* and *avaritiae*, but with a slightly different sense each time: 'shelter from the winter' and 'a home for greed'.

esse voluerunt – 'wished there to be'.

Chapter 40

age vero – 'come now' – this highlights the shift to the next of Pompeius' moral virtues – *temperantia*.

qua ... temperantia – descriptive ablative – 'what restraint [he has]'.

tantam celeritatem et tam incredibilem cursum – Cicero is referring again to the remarkable speed with which Pompeius conquered the pirates.

inventum – understand *esse. celeritatem* and *cursum* are both the subjects, but *inventum* agrees with the nearer.

gubernandi – genitive gerund after *ars* – 'skill in navigation'.

retardarunt – shortened form of *retardaverunt*.

signa et tabulas ceteraque ornamenta – the Romans were keen looters of Greek works of art, so 'souvenirs, pictures and other adornments'. This was seen as a bad thing when objects were stolen for the personal enrichment of the commanders, but the Romans seem to have been less judgemental when such objects were taken and donated to the Roman people at large, e.g., through temple dedication.

tollenda esse arbitrantur – 'think must be taken away'.

ea ... ille ... – both pronouns are emphatic.

Chapter 41

hac ... continentia – descriptive ablative after *fuisse* – 'Roman men had once this self-control'.

quod – 'something which …' – neuter because it refers to *the fact* that the Romans once had this self-control.

ea temperantia – descriptive ablative working with *magistratus* – 'magistrates of that restraint'.

ita faciles aditus – *aditus* as the subject of *esse dicuntur* and *faciles* as the complement – 'access is said to be so straightforward'; the same structure is used for *ita liberae querimoniae*.

privatorum – 'ordinary men' – i.e. men who did not hold a position on Pompeius' staff or in his household.

Chapter 42

Fairly swiftly, Cicero now deals with the remaining four moral virtues referred to in Chapter 36: *fides, facilitas* and *humanitas* are directly mentioned; *ingenium* is dealt with by reference to Pompeius' strategic insight (*consilio*) and his skill as an orator.

quantum + subjunctive – 'the extent to which …' – an indirect question dependent on *cognovistis*.

consilio … dicendi gravitate et copia valeat – *valeo* + ablative here; *consilio* – 'strategic insight'; *dicendi gravitate et copia* – 'the weight and the range of his rhetoric'.

in quo ipso – 'in which very skill' – *dicendi* is the antecedent.

hoc ipso ex loco – Cicero means the rostra, the speaker's platform from which he is addressing his audience (see Introduction, p. 1).

fidem – this word has been promoted for emphasis, but it is the accusative subject of *existimari,* and the antecedent of *quam*.

iudicarint – contracted form of *iudicaverint*; relative clause is causal, hence the subjunctive.

humanitate ... tanta est – another descriptive ablative – 'he has such great ...'.

difficile dictu – one of the most common uses of the supine is in its ablative case in phrases such as this – 'difficult to say'.

quin + subjunctive – 'that ...' – a common construction after verbs of doubting, and used when the verb of doubting is negative (or virtually negative – as here – since the question *quisquam dubitabit* expects the answer 'no').

tantum – 'great'.

videatur – subjunctive as part of the indirect speech following *dubitabit*.

Chapter 43

auctoritas – here begins the third section of the structure Cicero outlined in Chapter 28: the account of Pompeius' *auctoritas. auctoritas* was a key Roman concept – the power or influence which derived from a person's skills and achievements, rather than the power associated with a particular office or role.

multum – used as an adverb here – 'to a great extent'.

nemini dubium est – 'no one can doubt'.

quin + subjunctive – as in Chapter 42 – 'that ...' after a negative expression of doubt.

ea re – 'because of that very thing', i.e. the extent of Pompeius' *auctoritas.*

plurimum possit – 'has the greatest power'.

vehementer ... pertinere ... quid ... – *pertinere* is the infinitive (from the impersonal verb *pertinet*) in the indirect statement after *ignorat*; the questions introduced by *quid* depend on it: 'who is unaware that it is highly relevant what ...'.

cum sciamus homines ... commoveri – 'since we know that men ... are moved'. *ut aut contemnant ...* then follows *commoveri* – 'to scorn or to ...' *aut ... aut ...* – used for mutually exclusive alternatives.

opinione ... et fama – translate as *opinione et fama non minus quam....*

id quod – 'something which'.

iudicia – refers to the previous commands, to which Pompeius had been appointed by the Roman people's vote (see Introduction).

Chapter 44

an – encourages the answer 'no'.

quo – introduces a result clause, and is used in place of *ut eo*.

unum – 'alone'.

sibi – 'for themselves' – the dative shows that the election of Pompeius to be commander against the pirates was in the people's interest.

ut plura non dicam neque ... – *ut non ... neque ...* shows this to be a result clause, but in English translate as 'without saying ...'.

quantum – 'the extent to which'.

omnium rerum egregiarum – 'of every sort of excellence'.

quo die – 'on the day on which'.

tanta – picked up later by *quantum* and so 'as great a … as …'.

spe ac nomine – causal – 'because of the prospect and reputation'.

vix .. potuisset – 'scarcely could have …' – the pluperfect subjunctive used here for an unfulfilled statement about the past.

Chapter 45

Iam – marks the beginning of the next example of Pompeius' *auctoritas* and the power of his reputation.

in Ponto calamitate – the reference is to Chapter 25 of the speech and the defeat of Triarius (one of Lucullus' legates) at Zela in 67. Plutarch estimates that 7,000 Romans died, but Cicero exaggerates here when he says that Asia was in danger.

paulo ante – for *paulo antea* – 'a little earlier'.

amisissetis – an unfulfilled condition (notice *nisi*) – 'you would have lost'.

perfecturus – the future participle often – as here – has a meaning of 'likely to …' (and so too *conservaturus*).

aut – continues the indirect questions after *dubitabit*.

Vocabulary

ab (+ ablative)	**away from**
abditus -a -um	concealed, secret
absum, abesse, afui	I am absent
ac	and
accipio -cipere -cepi -ceptum	I receive
acer, acris, acre	keen, bitter, sharp
Achaia -ae, f	Achaea (a Roman province including all of Greece except Thessaly)
ad (+ accusative)	towards, to, for the purpose of
adeo -ire -ivi -itum	I go to
adfero, adferre, attuli, adlatum	I bring to
adimo -imere -emi -emptum	I take away
aditus -us, m	approach, access
adiungo -iungere -iunxi -iunctum	I join to
administra -ae, f	helper
administro -are	I manage, direct
admoneo -monere -monui -monitum	I remind, admonish
admurmuratio -onis, f	murmuring
adorno -are	I furnish, provide, adorn
adulescentia -ae, f	youth, young adulthood
adventus -us, m	arrival
aerarium -i, n	public treasury
aestas -atis, f	summer
Africa -ae, f	Africa
ager, agri, m	field, land
agnosco -noscere -novi -nitum	I recognise, admit, acknowledge

ago, agere, egi, actum	I set in motion, drive, do
alienus -a -um	of another
aliquis, aliquid	someone, something, anyone, anything
alius -a -ud	other, different
amicus -i, m	friend
amitto -mittere -misi -missum	I lose, let go
amo -are	I love
amoenitas -atis, f	pleasantness, charm
amplus -a -um	large, important, distinguished
an	or is it that …
animus -i, m	mind, heart
annona -ae, f	corn, provisions
annus -i, m	year
ante (+ accusative)	before, in front of
antea	before, previously
antiquitas -atis, f	antiquity, ancient times
apparo -are	I prepare, get ready
apud (+ accusative)	among
arbitror -ari	I think, judge
arma -orum, n pl	arms, weapons
ars, artis, f	art, skill
Asia -ae, f	Asia
atque	and
attenuo -are	I reduce
auctoritas -atis, f	authority, influence
audio, audire, audivi, auditum	I hear
aut … aut …	either … or …
autem	but
auxilium -i, n	help
avaritia -ae, f	greed

bello -are	**I wage war**
bellum -i, n	war
brevis -e	short
Brundisium -i, n	Brundisium
caelum -i, n	**the heavens, the sky**
Caieta -ae, f	Caieta
calamitas -atis, f	loss, misfortune
capio, capere, cepi, captum	I take, capture
caritas -atis, f	high price
causa -ae, f	case, cause, reason
celeber -bris -bre	filled, crowded
celeritas -atis, f	speed
celeriter	quickly
centuriatus -us, m	the office of centurion
certe	certainly, at any rate
certus -a -um	fixed, certain
ceteri -ae -a	the rest
Cilicia -ae, f	Cilicia (a region in Asia Minor)
cingo, cingere, cinxi, cinctum	I surround, encircle
civilis -e	relating to / of a citizen, civic / civil
civis -is, m/f	citizen
civitas -atis, f	state
clarus -a -um	clear, distinguished, bright
classis -is, f	fleet
claudo, claudere, clausi, clausum	I shut, close off
Cnidus -i, f	Cnidus
cogito -are	I think, consider
cognitio -onis, f	getting to know, study, acquaintance with

cognosco -gnoscere -gnovi -gnitum	I learn, get to know
Colophon -onis, f	Colophon
comes -itis, m/f	companion
commemoro -are	I call to mind, mention
committo -mittere -misi -missum	I bring together, I entrust, I commit
communis -e	common, shared
compleo -plere -plevi -pletum	I fill up
concerto -are	I strive (against), I dispute
concupisco -piscere -pivi -pitum	I desire eagerly
conficio -ficere -feci -fectum	I make ready, I obtain, I bring to an end
confirmo -are	I strengthen
confiteor -fiteri- fessus sum	I admit, confess
confligo -fligere -flixi -flictum	I come into conflict with
consequor -sequi -secutus sum	I go after, obtain
conservo -are	I keep, preserve, maintain
considero -are	I regard carefully, consider
consilium -i, n	plan-making, plan, strategy
conspicio -spicere -spexi -spectum	I catch sight of, see
contemno -temnere -tempsi -temptum	I despise
contentio -onis, f	comparison
continentia -ae, f	self-control, restraint
contineo -tinere -tinui -tentum	I contain, restrain
copia -ae, f	abundance
copiae -arum, f pl	military forces
cotidie	every day
credo, credere, credidi, creditum	I believe
cresco, crescere, crevi, cretum	I grow, increase

Cretensis -e	Cretan, of Crete
cum (+ ablative)	with
cum (+ subjunctive)	since, although, when
cupiditas -atis, f	greed, ambition
cupio, cupere, cupivi, cupitum	I desire
cursus -us, m	journey, a march
de (+ ablative)	**about**
debeo, debere, debui, debitum	I owe, I ought
declaro, declarare	I reveal, make clear, declare
deditio -onis, f	surrender
dedo, dedere, dedidi, deditum	I give up, surrender
defendo -fendere -fendi -fensum	I defend, ward off
delabor -labi -lapsus sum	I glide / fall down from
delectatio -onis, f	delight, pleasure
deleo, delere, delevi, deletum	I destroy, blot out
deliberatio -onis, f	consideration, decision
deligo, deligere, delegi, delectum	I pick, choose
denique	at last, further, finally, in short
deposco -poscere -poposci	I demand, ask for
deprecator -oris, m	one that pleads for, an advocate
depromo -promere -prompsi -promptum	I take out
desero -serere -serui -sertum	I desert, abandon, neglect
desertus -a -um	abandoned, deserted
devoco -are	I call down / away from
dico, dicere, dixi, dictum	I say, speak
dies -ei, m	day
difficilis -e	difficult
dignitas -atis, f	worth, merit, reputation
dignus -a -um (+ ablative)	worthy of

diligo -ligere -lexi -lectum	I choose, love, esteem highly
diripio -ripere -ripui -reptum	I snatch away
disciplina -ae, f	teaching, education, study
discrimen -inis, n	critical moment, turning point
dispergo -spergere -spersi -spersum	I scatter
diuturnus -a -um	long-lasting
diversus -a -um	different
divido -videre -visi -visum	I divide up, separate into parts
divinitus	divinely, by the power of the gods
divinus -a -um	belonging to the gods, godly
domus -us, f	home
dubito -are	I doubt, I am uncertain
dubium -i, n	doubt
dubius -a -um	doubtful, doubting
duco, ducere, duxi, ductum	I draw (off / away), lead, take
duo, duae, duo	two
duodecim	twelve
dux, ducis, m	leader
e, ex (+ ablative)	**from, out of**
efficio -ficere -feci -fectum	I make, produce, bring it about that …
ego	I
egregius -a -um	excellent, extraordinary
enim	for
eo	thither, to there
eruditus -a -um	learned, educated, trained
et	and, also, even
excello -ere	I excel, stand out, be better than someone (+ dative)
exemplum -i, n	example

exerceo, exercere, exercui, exercitum	I make strong, exercise, train
exercitus -us, m	army
eximius -a -um	exceptional, distinguished
existimo -are	I judge, consider, value, regard
expeto -petere -petivi -petitum	I strive after, seek, demand
explico -are	I disentangle
exploro -are	I search out, explore
exspectatio -onis, f	a waiting for, expectation
exterus -a -um	foreign
extremus -a -um	last, end of, outermost
facilis -e	**easy**
facilitas -atis, f	ease, friendliness
facio, facere, feci, factum	I do, make
falsum -i, n	mistake
fama -ae, f	reputation, rumour, public opinion
felicitas -atis, f	good fortune, success
fero, ferre, tuli, latum	I carry, bear
fides -ei, f	loyalty
fio, fieri, factus sum	I happen, become
firmus -a -um	strong, firm
fortis -e	strong, powerful, courageous
fortitudo -inis, f	strength, bravery, courage
fortuna -ae, f	fortune, fate, luck
forum -i, n	forum
frumentarius -a -um	relating to the corn supply
fugio, fugere, fugi, fugitum	I flee, escape
Galli -orum, m pl	**Gauls**
Gallia -ae, f	Gaul
gens, gentis, f	clan / tribe, people

genus, generis, n	type, variety, sort
gero, gerere, gessi, gestum	I do, conduct, wage (war)
gloria -ae, f	glory
Graecia -ae, f	Greece
gravitas -atis, f	weight, importance, authority
guberno -are	I steer a ship, I am a helmsman
habeo, habere, habui, habitum	**I have, hold**
hiberna -orum, n pl	winter quarters
hiberno -are	I spend the winter
hic, haec, hoc	this
hiems -is, f	winter
Hispania -ae, f	Spain
homo, hominis, m	man, human
hostis, hostis, m	enemy
humanitas -atis, f	humanity, kindness
iam	**now**
idem, eadem, idem	the same, also
igitur	therefore
ignominia -ae, f	dishonour, disgrace
ignoro -are	I do not know
ille, illa, illud	that
Illyricus -a -um	Illyrian (the Illyriii were a people living near the Adriatic sea, in the modern Yugoslavia and Albania)
imminuo -uere –ui -utum	I lessen, diminish
imperator -oris, m	commander
imperatorius -ae -a	belonging to a general
imperium -i, n	command, power, empire
impero -are	I command, order
impetus -us, m	onset, impulse, attack

in (+ ablative)	in
inauditus -a -um	unheard (of), unusual
incipio -cipere -cepi -ceptum	I begin
incommodum -i, n	disadvantage, misfortune
incredibilis -e	not to be believed, incredible
inde	from there, then
industria -ae, f	diligence
ineo -ire -i(v)i -itum	I come in, enter upon, begin
infimus -a -um	lowest
inflatus -a -um	puffed up, pompous
ingenium -i, n	natural talent
inimicus -a -um	enemy
iniuria -ae, f	injury, injustice
innocens, innocentis	innocent, blameless
innocentia -ae, f	integrity
innumerabilis -e	uncountable
inopia -ae, f	lack, scarcity
insolitus -a -um	unaccustomed, unusual
inspecto -are	I look at, observe
instituo, instituere, institui, institutum	I put in place, establish, undertake
insula -ae, f	island
insum -esse -fui	I am in / on, I belong
intellego -legere -lexi -lectum	I understand
inter (+ accusative)	among
interficio -ficere -feci -fectum	I kill
internicio -onis, f	slaughter, massacre
intueor -tueri -tuitus sum	I gaze at, consider
invenio, invenire, inveni, inventum	I find
invitus -a -um	unwilling
ipse, ipsa, ipsum	*emphatic* -self, very own

irascor, irasci, iratus sum	I grow angry
is, ea, id	he, she, it, that, this
ita	in such a way, in this way, thus
Italia -ae, f	Italy
itaque	and so, therefore
item	likewise
iter, itineris, n	journey, route
iterum	again
iudex -icis, m	judge
iudicium -i, n	judgement
iudico -are	I judge
labes -is, f	**stain, disgrace**
labor -oris, m	hard work
lateo -ere	I lie hidden, I am unknown
latus -a -um	wide
legatus -i, m	legate, deputy, ambassador
legio -onis, f	legion
lego, legere, legi, lectum	I read
liber, libera, liberum	free, free from
liberi -orum, m pl	children
libero -are	I set free
libido -inis, f	violent desire, passion, longing
litterae -arum, f pl	letter
locus -i, m	place
longe	at a distance, far from
longinquus -a -um	long, at length, far away
longus -a -um	long
ludus -i, m	play, game, school
lux, lucis, f	light, salvation
magis	**more**
magistratus -us, m	magistrate, official

magnitudo, magnitudinis, f	(great) size, magnitude
magnus -a -um	big
maiores -um, pl	ancestors
malo, malle, malui	I prefer
mansuetudo -inis, f	gentleness
manus -us, f	hand, (armed) band of men
mare -is, n	sea
maritimus -a -um	of the sea
maximus -a -um	greatest (superlative of magnus)
medius -a -um	middle of
memoria -ae, f	memory, recollection
mercator -oris, m	merchant
metuo, metuere, metui, metutum	I fear
metus -us, m	fear
miles, militis, m	soldier
militaris -e	military
militia -ae, f	military service, warfare
minito -are (+ dative)	I threaten (frequentative)
minus	less
miror -ari	I admire
Misenum -i, n	Misenum
Mithridates -is	Mithridates (king of Pontus)
mitto, mittere, misi, missum	I send
modo	only, just
mors, mortis, f	death
multus -a -um	much (plural = many)
munio, munire, munivi, munitum	I fortify
nascor, nasci, natus sum	**I am born**
natio -onis, f	nation, people
navalis -e	of ships, naval
navigo -are	I sail

navis, navis, f	ship
-ne	?
ne ... quidem	not even
necessarius -a -um	necessary
negotium -i, n	transaction, task, employment
nemo, neminis	no one
neque	and ... not
neque ... neque ...	neither ... nor ...
nisi	if not, unless
nobilis -e	famous, noble
nobilitas -atis, f	fame, celebrity, excellence
noceo, nocere, nocui, nocitum (+ dative)	I injure, harm
nomen -inis, n	name
nomino -are	I name
non	not
non modo ... sed etiam	not only ... but even ...
nondum	not yet
noster, nostra, nostrum	our
novus -a -um	new, novel
nullus -a -um	none, no, not any
numerus -i, m	number
numquam	never
nunc	now
obeo -ire -ivi -itum	**I go to, enter upon, carry out**
obses, obsidis, m/f	hostage
Oceanus -i, m	the Ocean (the sea that surrounds the earth)
odi, odisse	I hate, destest
offensio -onis, f	misfortune, setback
omnis -e	all, every

opinio -onis, f	opinion
oportet, oportere, oportuit	it behoves, one should
oppidum -i, n	town
opprimo -primere -pressi -pressum	I press upon, crush
ops, opis, f	means, power, resources
ora -ae, f	boundary, coastline, region
oratio -onis, f	speech, language, eloquence
orbis, orbis, m	circle, globe
orbis terrarum	the world
ornamentum -i, n	decoration, embellishment
Ostiensis -e	at Ostia / relating to Ostia
ostium -i, n	entrance, mouth
paco -are	**I pacify, make peaceful**
Pamphylia -ae, f	Pamphylia (a district in Asia Minor between Cilicia and Lycia)
par, paris (+ dative)	equal to
partim	partly
patefacio -facere -feci -factum	I open up, make accessible
pater, patris, m	father
paulum -i, n	a little
pax, pacis, f	peace
pecunia -ae, f	money
per (+ accusative)	through
perfectus -a -um	perfect, complete
perfero -ferre -tuli -latum	I deliver
perficio -ficere -feci -fectum	I complete, finish, accomplish
perfugium -i, n	refuge
periculosus -a -um	dangerous
periculum -i, n	danger

permitto -mittere -misi -missum (+ dative)	I allow
pertimesco -timescere -timui	I am very much afraid of
pertineo -tinere -tinui	I reach to, I am relevant to
pervado -vadere -vasi -vasum	I go through, I spread to
pervenio -venire -veni -ventum	I arrive at, come into
plenus -a -um (+ genitive)	full of
plus, pluris	more
pono, ponere, posui, positum	I place, put
Pontus -i, m	the Black Sea
populus -i, m	people, community, nation
portus -us, m	harbour
possum, posse, potui	I am able
postremo	at last
potestas -atis, f	power
potissimus -a -um	best of all
praeceptum -i, n	command, instruction
praeclarus -a -um	very bright, very distinguished, excellent
praeda -ae, f	plunder, spoils of war
praedo -onis, m	plunderer, pirate
praeficio, praeficere, praefeci, praefectum	I put x (acc) in charge of y (dat)
praepono -ponere -posui -positum	I put x (acc) in charge of y (dat)
praesidium -i, n	military garrison, protection
praetereo -ire -ivi -itum	I pass over, pass by
praetor -oris, m	praetor (Roman magistrate)
premo, premere, pressi, pressum	I press upon, pursue, squeeze
primum	at first
princeps, principis, m	leader, of first rank

privatus -i, m	a private / ordinary person (i.e., not connected to the imperial household)
prodo, prodere, prodidi, proditum	I bring forth, I betray
proelium -i, n	battle
proficiscor, proficisci, profectus sum	I set out, proceed
prope	nearby, near
prope (+ accusative)	near
proprius -a -um (+ genitive)	one's own, characteristic of
propter (+ accusative)	on account of
propugnaculum -i, n	fortification, protection, defence
prosterno -sternere -stravi -stratum	I cast down, destroy
provideo -videre -vidi -visum	I see at a distance, foresee, take precautions
provincia -ae, f	province
pueritia -ae, f	boyhood
pugno -are	I fight
puto -are	I think, consider
quaero, quaerere, quaesivi/ quaesii, quaesitum	**I seek, search for**
quaestus -us, m	profit
qualis -e	of what sort
quam	than
quamquam	although
quantus -a -um	how great, of what size
quare	for which reason, why
quattuor	four
quem ad modum	in what manner, how
querimonia -ae, f	complaint
queror, queri, questus sum	I complain, lament

qui, quae, quod	who, which
quidam, quaedam, quoddam	a certain
quies -etis, f	rest, sleep
quin	that
Quirites -um, m pl	citizens of Rome
quis, quid	who, what, which
quisquam, quaequam, quicquam	anyone, anything
quo	to where, whither
quocumque	to what point, whithersoever
quondam	once, at a certain time
quoniam	since
quoque	also

ratio -onis, f	**rational account, calculation**
recipio -cipere -cepi -ceptum	I take back, receive
recordor -ari	I remember, think over
redimo -imere -emi -emptum	I buy back, I ransom
redundo -are	I overflow with
refertus -a -um (+ genitive)	crammed full
regio -onis, f	region
relinquo -linquere -liqui -lictum	I leave behind, abandon
reliquus -a -um	remaining, the other, (in plural) the rest
remex, remigis, m	rower
remoror -ari	I slow down, hinder
repente	suddenly
res, rei, f	thing, matter, circumstance, affair
res frumentaria	the corn supply
res publica, rei publicae, f	the state, the Roman Republic
resto, restare, restiti	I remain
retardo -are	I slow down, impede

Romanus -a -um	Roman
rumor -oris, m	rumour, common talk, hearsay
saepe	**often**
Samus -i, f	Samos
sanctus -a -um	holy, virtuous, blameless
sanguis -inis, m	blood
Sardinia -ae, f	Sardinia
satis	enough, sufficiently
sciens, scientis	knowing, knowledgeable
scientia -ae, f	knowledge
scio, scire, scivi, scitum	I know, understand
se	him / her / it, himself / herself / itself
se recipere	to retreat
securis -is, m	axe (symbols of the power of the highest magistrates in Rome)
sed	but
sepelio -pelire -pelivi -pultum	I bury
sermo -onis, m	conversation
servilis -e	relating to / of a slave
servio, servire (+ dative)	I am a slave to
servitus -utis, f	slavery
severus -a -um	strict
sic	thus, in such a way, in this way
Sicilia -ae, f	Sicily
sicut	just as
signum -i, n	sign, military standard, token
sine (+ ablative)	without
singulus -a -um	single, separate, one at a time
sinus -us, m	bay, gulf
socius -a -um	ally

soleo -ere, solitus sum	I am accustomed
solus -a -um	alone, only
spes -ei, f	hope
spiritus -us, m	breath, life
splendor -oris, m	brilliance, distinction
statuo -uere -ui -utum	I establish, decide
stipendium -i, n	tax, pay, period of military service
studium -i, n	enthusiasm, zeal
subsidium -i, n	help, support
sum, esse, fui, futurus (future participle)	I am
summus -a -um	greatest, highest, most important
sumo, sumere, sumpsi, sumptum	I take, choose
sumptus -us, m	expense
supero, superare, superavi, superatum	I overpower, I surpass
suscipio -cipere -cepi -ceptum	I undertake, begin
suus -a -um	his / her / its own
tabula -ae, f	**writing tablet, document, picture**
taeter -tra -trum	foul, offensive, hideous
tam	so
tamen	even so, nevertheless
tantum	so much, to such an extent
tantus -a -um	so big, so great
tecta -orum, n pl	roofs, buildings
temperantia -ae, f	restraint
tempestivus -a -um	seasonable, happening at the right time
templum -i, n	temple

tempus -oris, n	time, period of time
teneo, tenere, tenui, tentum	I hold, hold fast
terra -ae, f	land
terror -oris, m	fear, terror
testis -is m/f	witness
Tiberinus -a -um	of the River Tiber
Tigranes -is	Tigranes (king of Armenia, and son-in-law and ally of Mithridates)
timeo -ere -ui	I am afraid, fear
tollo, tollere, sustuli, sublatum	I lift up, I remove
totus -a -um	whole, entire
Transalpinus -a -um	beyond the Alps, Transalpine (Gaul)
transmitto -mittere -misi -missum	I send across, I go across
tres, tria	three
triumphus -i, m	triumph, triumphal procession
tum	then
turpis -e	foul, shameful
tutus -a -um	safe
ubertas -atis, f	**abundance, fruitfulness**
ubique	everywhere
ullus -a -um	any
ultimus -a -um	furthest
umquam	ever
unde	from where
undequinquagesimus -a -um	forty-ninth
undique	from all sides
universus -a -um	altogether, whole
unus -a -um	one, only one
urbs, urbis, f	city

usque	all the way
usus -us, m	use, practice, skill
ut (+ indicative)	when, as, since, how
ut (+ subjunctive)	that, in order to, to
utinam (+ subjunctive)	introduces a wish – would that …
utrum … an …	whether … or …
valeo -ere	**I am strong**
varius -a -um	various, changeable
vectigal -alis, n	revenue, tax
vehementer	powerfully, exceedingly
veneo, venire, venii, venitum	I am for sale
venio, venire, veni, ventum	I come
ventus -i, m	wind
ver, veris, n	spring
verbum -i, n	word
vero	indeed, really, in truth
vester, vestra, vestrum	your
vestigium -i, n	footstep, trace
vetus, veteris	old, long-lasting
victor -oris, m	winner
victoria -ae, f	victory
video, videre, vidi, visum	I see
videor, videri, visus sum	I seem
vilitas -atis, f	cheapness
vinco, vincere, vici, victum	I defeat
vir, viri, m	man
virtus, virtutis, f	manly excellence, courage, virtue
vis, vim (acc), vi (abl)	force, violence
viso, visere, visi, visum	I look at carefully, go to see
vita -ae, f	life, livelihood
vix	scarcely, hardly

volo, velle, volui	I am willing, wish
voluptas -atis, f	(sensual) pleasure
vos	you (pl)
vulgus -i, n	the people, the crowd, the mob